# Loom Knitting Guide & Patterns

## Perfect for Beginner to Advanced Loom Knitters!

Learn basics, find valuable reference information, see knitting math explained, and get the most out of your knitting skills including chart reading and needle pattern converting.  Multiple patterns are included.

### KRISTEN MANGUS
#### GoodKnit Kisses

**Loom Knitting Guide & Patterns**
**Perfect for Beginner to Advanced Loom Knitters**
Kristen Mangus
GoodKnit Kisses

Book Design First Edition by Lindsey Murrary
Second Edition by Kristen Mangus
Photography by Kristen Mangus, Calvin Hon, Carol Blakeley
Graphics by Kristen Mangus, Lindsey Murrary, Charity Windham
Covers by Lindsey Murray
Models - Crystal Clark, Morgan Mangus, and Megan Mangus

The title is available as a printed book and an ebook.

PUBLISHED BY:
GoodKnit Kisses

REQUESTS FOR INFORMATION:
GoodKnit Kisses
PO Box 90
Keller, TX 76244

Printed in the United States of America.

Second Edition 2016

Book:     ISBN 978-0-9976329-1-0
eBook:    ISBN 978-0-9976329-2-7

goodknitkisses.com

youtube.com/goodknitkisses

# Table of Contents

# Introduction

Welcome to the world of Loom Knitting! Knitting without needles is a great way to knit an amazing array of projects. From tiny stitches in a sock to jumbo stitches for a bulky blanket, you can enjoy making all kinds of knitwear and accessories until your heart's content.

Knitting on a loom is like knitting without needles because each peg works as a needle with less chance of a dropped stitch. Loom Knitting is especially helpful for people with hand or limb dexterity challenges and other health concerns that would be otherwise impossible/difficult with needles. Loom Knitting is relaxing but also exercises the brain! Many people start with hats or scarves but can learn to knit detailed projects, too!

In this book you will learn basics, find valuable reference information, math explained, and simply find how to get the most out of your knitting skills. Learn abbreviations and their meanings, stitches explained, how to work stitches, and patterns to get you started. Skills for this book range from absolute Beginner to Advanced loom knitters. If you have already loomed before feel free to dive right in or visit **Loom Basics** Chapter 1 to get a jump-start on learning. Intermediate and advanced loom knitters will find valuable reference materials in **Knitter's Math and Charts** Chapter 5.

I'm excited to have put together a valuable chart on looms listed in their gauge, with suggested needle ranges, including suggested yarn weight, stitches per inch ranges and even the right crochet hook to go with it all. Metric numbers are also included for the UK/AU standard for yarn. This was a true labor of love and dedicated a whole Chapter (4) on **Gauge**! Also found here I'll teach you **How to Read Patterns and Charts** (Chapter 2), convert a needle pattern with a handy reference chart, and calculate formulas for how much yarn you need or how many stitches to cast-on! Check out **Tips and Techniques** in Chapter 3 for even more!

I suggest reading the book first before jumping into the patterns so you can learn the loom and the new language of knitting. Read a few times and look at any step-by-step pictures or video links to get the best understanding when trying something new.

**For video instructions please click the underlined hyperlink in the eBook** explanation after reading. **For the printed book use the number after the underlines word(s) and reference our Endnote List for the link.** Endnotes can also be found in hyperlink version on the website at the following address. http://www.goodknitkisses.com/Resources/loom-knitting-guide-and-patterns-2016/[1]

Happy Looming! -Kristen

# Author's Acknowledgments

A special thanks to editors Carol Blakeley at Lily Dot Designs and Kelly Jones at Kiss-Looms; special permissions and partnerships with Staci Perry at VeryPinkKnits, Stasia Neal-Renfrow at LoomKnittingCentral, Brenda Myers at Loom Lore, Charity Windham, Kelsey Millburn at Vintage Storehouse, Alles Hutchinson, Joann Fernstrom and Yarn Craft Council. Thank you Carol for your administrative and editorial support for GKK, your friendship and partnership have been a lifeline for me. You are a treasure! Thank you to Niki Schertz as well for GKK support, your social media team support over the last few years have been a god-send. I treasure our friendship as well and am so happy to wish you well on your new journey in motherhood, you are a wonderful mother!

Test Knitters for patterns in this book: Calvin Hon, Terri Deese, Denice Johnson, Tammy Anderson, Joanna Brandt, Charity Windham, Luisa Mangus, Niki Schertz, and Carol Blakeley.

Models: Crystal Clark, Morgan Mangus, and Megan Mangus.

Loom manufactures for their input and personal help on our gauge chart: Kelly Jones at Kiss-Looms, Cindy Clyde and Kristy Hunter at CinDwood Looms, Kim Novak at Knitting Board, Boye, and Horizon Group. And special thanks to original inspiration and encouragement with Stasia Neal-Renfrow; thank you Stasia for your outstanding contributions to the Loom Knitting community and for your personal loom collection sent to GKK to teach and inspire future generations!

To Michael Sellick, of The Crochet Crowd, for always believing, encouraging and inspiring me. You were there in the beginning and we partnered so well. From hosting our Retreat together to helping on each other's YouTube channels it has been a privilege to work with you. Thank you for all the sage advice and above all your friendship.

Above all thank you to God for the talent and faithfulness to do this, the name GoodKnit Kisses and for saving me through post-partem with this craft! To my incredible husband, John, thank you for your love and support with this crazy new adventure for the last 5 years. If you didn't support me I wouldn't still be plugging away. To our three beautiful children thank you for your overwhelming enthusiasm for anything I make and let me stay silly with the not so great ones, too! I love my creative and silly family. You are what matters most. Thank you for your support and love!

To friends, fans, followers and more test knitters on other projects: Over the last five years has been quite a journey. Thank you for everything. You cheering me on to write my own book finally has been realized into being and has been a true labor of love. You continue to inspire and encourage me everyday!

Love,
Kristen

# Chapter 1

**Using your Loom**:
Looms are used to knit flat panels (single knit), double knit panels and circular pieces like a tube. The projects in here will give you a chance to work both flat and circular pieces as well as beginner stitches and techniques to help you grow your skills. Looms come in various sizes and peg spacing. Many of the stitches and techniques discussed for one brand can still be knit on most any loom. Don't worry about having every loom; work with what you have and have fun. Loom knitting fever will hit and your collection will grow along with your skills and desires!

I have put together an exciting book for you! Please read instructions and tips before starting. Also included are Easy and Intermediate patterns to master. Try the **Chic Retreat Cowl** later, in Chapter 6, as a stitch sampler! Many of the terms, stitches and even full patterns called for in this book I have a video for your convenience. Be sure to click technique links to videos for a real-time understanding of each step as you go.

*A quick start-up tip! Your knitting all falls on the inside of the loom and comes out the bottom of the loom. The **Right Side** of the fabric faces out.*

In this chapter we'll give a quick overview, jump into abbreviations, show definitions, followed by a section dedicated to **First Hats**. In this section we'll walk through a basic hat and types of brim styles to choose from for your first hat.

**Overview on Loom Sizes and Gauge**:
A knitting loom will make a knitted fabric out of yarn. On the knitted fabric, the space or gaps between the pegs on the loom makes the stitches larger or smaller; this is called the *knitting gauge*. The knitting gauge is determined by the yarn chosen, loom gauge, stitch chosen and the loom knitter's tension (tightness). For more details see **Gauge** Chapter 4.

**Overview on Reading Written and Charted Patterns**:
The patterns here will have instructions written out. Many times rows are repeated but it saves space to tell you to repeat those rows again. To help show you what the project looks like there are charts sometimes in patterns. Charts also appear in needle patterns and are great ways to convert to loom knitting, as all show graphically the "Right Side" or RS of the knitting like a loom knit project. See **Reading Charts** in Chapter 2 for more.

## Abbreviations

In a pattern, it is necessary to abbreviate loom knitting stitches or any kind of knitting or crochet for that matter. It condenses the pattern down making it shorter to read. After you are used to loom knit abbreviations, it will be second nature to read and remember.

Before starting any knitting pattern, **always** read all notes and abbreviations in the pattern first. A designer may note that all knit stitches (frequently made 1 of 4 different ways) be made a certain way. The abbreviation **K** might be used to Knit the stitch but it could mean to knit how the designer wrote in their notes. When in doubt use a loose U-Knit stitch, study the photos, or ask the designer.

We have compiled the following to help you reference what the loom knit abbreviations mean. Written instructions are found later in this book for many of these terms.

**For video instructions please click the underlined hyperlink in the eBook. For the printed book use the number after the underlines word(s) and reference our Endnote List for the link.** Endnotes can also be found in hyperlink version on the website at the following address. http://www.goodknitkisses.com/Resources/loom-knitting-guide-and-patterns-2016/

approx = approximately
beg = begin(s)(ning)
bet = between
BO = bind off[2]
btwn = between
C1B = Cable 1 back (cables 2 stitches)
C1F = Cable 1 front (cables 2 stitches)
C2B = Cable 2 back (cables 4 stitches)
C2F = Cable 2 front (cables 4 stitches)
C3B = Cable 3 back (cables 6 stitches)
C3F = Cable 3 front (cables 6 stitches)
CBS = Chunky Braid Stitch
CC = contrasting color
cn = cable needle[3]
CO = cast on[4]
cont = continu(e)(s)(ing)
dbl = double
dec = decreas(e)(s)(ing)[5] - there are different types
DLS = Diamond Lace Stitch (aka flat Fig 8 stitch)[6]
DS = Double Stitch
EW = e-wrap, also k1tbl (knit one in the back loop, also twisted knit)[7]
F = flat knit[8]

FK = flat knit[9]
inc = increas(e)(s)(ing)[10] - there are different types
K = knit[11]
K1b = knit 1 in the row below.
K1b = knit through the back loop (also K1tbl) = same as an e-wrap (EW)[12]
K2tog = knit 2 together[13]
K2togb = Knit 2 stitches together through back loop (is k2tog using ew stitch).
K3tog = knit 3 together
K3togb = Knit 3 stitches together through back loop (is k3tog using ew stitch).
Kfb = knit in front and back of st.
lp st = loop stitch
lp(s) = loop(s)
M1 = make 1
M2 = make two
MC = main color
meas = measure(s)1[14]
ndl(s) = needle(s)
opp = opposite
p = purl[15]
P1b = purl through the back loop (purl as usual but twist when replacing loop).
P2sso = pass 2 slipped sts over.
P2tog = purl 2 together.
P2togb = purl 2 together in back (purl 2tog as usual but twist when replacing loop).
P3tog = purl 3 together.
Pm = place marker
Psso = pass slipped stitch over.
PU = pick up
rem = remain(s)(ing)
rep = repeat(s)(ing)
rev = revers(e)(ing)
Rev St st = reverse stockinette stitch (purl side is right side)[16].
rf = right front
RH = right hand
rnd(s) = round(s)
RS = right side
S2KP or S2KP2 = slip 2 stitches together, knit 1, pass two slipped stitches over.
Sk = skip
Sk2p = Slip 1, k2tog, pass sl st over.
Skp = slip 1, knit 1, pass slipped stitch over.
Sl = slip
Sl st = slip stitch
Slip1-k1-psso = slip 1, knit 1, pass slip stitch over.
SM = slip marker
sp(s) = space(s)
Ssk = slip, slip, knit

Ssp = slip, slip, purl[17]
St st = Stockinette stitch[18]
st(s) = stitch(es)
Tbl = through the back loop[19] (Twisted stitch same as EW; P tbl just twist after)
Tog = together
Work even
WS = wrong side
Wyib = with yarn in back
Wyif = with yarn in front
YO= yarn over[20]

**QUICK START TECHNIQUES**:
Casting On (See Basic Terms and Getting Started)
In the Round (Circular Knitting)
Flat Panel Knitting and Slipped Stitch Method
E-Wrap Cast On and Tight E-Wrap Cast On
Double Stitch Cast On
Garter Stitch Pattern
Basic (Flat Panel) Bind Off
Hemmed Brim
Drawstring (Gather) Bind Off
Whipstitch, Weaving and I-cords

**Basic Terms and How to Get Started:**
Casting on is the way to start knitting and get loops of yarn on a loom. In a pattern you may also see the abbreviation CO which also means Cast On. To get different edges or the look at designer wants, there are different ways to CO. Some are stiff or stretchy, others bend the stitch to the front or back, and some are functional or even decorative. As you can see, there are many ways to CO and you'll see a few listed here. The pegs on a loom are like short knitting needles. As yarn gets pulled from the ball onto the loom we call that yarn the Working Yarn. As yarn is worked onto the pegs, we call these stitches; they make up a whole knitted fabric. When stitches are still on the peg you may see them called loops but they're still stitches. Taking the stitches off the loom to finish is called binding off (BO) or casting off. There are many ways to BO. To finish a knit project, weave the tail ends or sew edges with yarn and a tapestry needle.

Read further down for stitches, terms and techniques. For a quick start project see **QUICK HAT**.

**QUICK START HAT:** Use instructions here to make a hat and learn new skills. Look at terms shown in *CAPS*. (For more info on basic hat techniques and sizes see **Hat Chart** in **Knitter's Math and Charts** Chapter 5). This is a good practice project before diving into a pattern; more detailed hat information and charts can be found in the book.
   1. Use 1 strand of worsted weight yarn and tie a **SLIPKNOT**.

2. Place on anchor peg or starting peg of round loom (or small "long loom").
3. **E-WRAP CAST ON** all stitches working to the left (clockwise direction) IN THE ROUND.  If left-handed, you may prefer to work to the right.
4. Continue knitting in the E-Wrap stitch for 2 inches. (Make HEMMED BRIM[21] or continue)
5. Continue knitting until hat measures 6 1/2 inches (Baby - see HAT CHART) to brim edge; if skipped "hemmed brim" a rolled brim will appear.
6. **GATHERED BIND OFF**. Your first hat is complete.

**TIPS:** *With the e-wrap stitch you will see it is looser and stretchy. Use DS or FK for tighter stitch or use thicker yarn. For a less bulky hat crown use* Modified Gathered Bind[22] *off and hat tips found in this book.*

*TROUBLESHOOTING GUIDE:*
- *If knitting is too tight try knitting one stitch at a time instead of wrapping entire loom. If e-wrapping stitches, use a yarn guide which can also help ease tension.  In a pinch, a hollowed out pen can be used to guide the yarn and keep your fingers from pulling the yarn too tightly around the pegs. Another way to loosen up is to tug on the stitch, on the peg, after it is knit. This loosens the stitch for the next row. If your stitches remain too tight your gauge would yield more stitches per inch (or cm) than needed and your project could become too small.*
- *If loops are too loose then your gauge could be off which can cause your project to be too large. Another risk is the loop could easily pop off the peg when the loom is moved or stored. To prevent this only work enough yarn around the peg to clear the top of the peg. The loop should move freely but snug enough not to pop off or "fall" off the peg.*
- *Some patterns may read to work clockwise or counter-clockwise. Most don't matter so knit as comfortable. If the pattern DOES call for a direction then work that direction as the stitch pattern could change the look.*

# Glossary and Terms Continued

<u>SLIPKNOT</u>:[23]

A way to tie on, or anchor yarn to the loom; place it on anchor or first peg after slipknot made. There are multiple ways to make a **slipknot**. Try this one way. Take the strand and wrap it twice around your finger letting a 6-inch tail hang toward the end of your finger. Take the back loop and place slightly in front of the loop toward the end of your finger. Now take the new back loop and pass it over the top of the new front loop and pull over the tip of your finger. Tighten by pulling a strand get the slack out. Place on starter or 1st peg.

**IN THE ROUND (CIRCULAR KNITTING):**

Knitting "in-the-round" means to knit in a circle or circular direction; making rounds of knitting as you work. The knitting will become a tube. Working your knitting in the round usually can go in either direction, unless a pattern says different, but you must keep going the same direction. The loom can be shaped as a circle, rectangle or other shapes as long as the pegs are spaced so the knitting will have evenly spaced stitches and connect in a complete circuit.

*<u>TIP</u>[24]: If the pattern does not state direction, and you have several purl stitches, work circular knitting to the left if you're right-handed (clockwise) and to the right if left-handed; a comfortable direction.*

<u>FLAT PANEL KNITTING</u>:[25]

Working back and forth from left-to-right and then right-to-left to make a panel of stitches. Or to explain differently, knitting in one direction then turning to knit in the opposite direction without joining the first and last stitches. This creates a flat panel that is not a tube. A circular loom can make a flat panel but the first and last pegs will not get connected. Working all the stitches on the pegs can create a bump on the edges to be used to sew edges together with yarn; this is called the selvedge edge. For a cleaner looking edge used **Slipped Stitch Method**.

<u>SLIPPED STITCH METHOD</u>:[26]

Flat Panel with edge of neat v-shaped stitches on each edge of your piece. This method should be used when the edge will be seen. To slip the stitch, simply start the row by not working the first peg by moving the yarn between the 1st and 2nd peg and start working the 2nd peg of that row. The 2nd peg will be whatever stitch is written in the pattern. Sometimes slipping is called skipping the stitch.

<u>E-WRAP STITCH (EW)</u>:[27]

E-wrap stitches are twisted knit stitches; wrapped on a loom they look like cursive "e". They do not lay down flat like a standard knit, shaped like a "V", but are more stretchy and easy for the beginner. The EW stitch lays more like a "Y" shape in the knitting. An EW stitch can work clockwise or counter clockwise on the loom, it doesn't matter which way except make sure your round (row) is always in the same direction. To EW a peg move your yarn to the back of the peg (opposite side of the groove-side) and wrap around the front of that peg, then back to the back again around the loom. Make sure your yarn crosses at the back of the peg like a small cursive "e".

**LIFELINE (and use as PROVISIONAL BIND OFF):**
Extra yarn placed through a row or series of stitches. This helps if you drop stitches or need to knit backwards  (**tink = knit spelled backwards**) to fix a problem.  Also helps if stitches should be held for later.  Use a smooth and contrasting color yarn to see and work stitches easier. (Video link[28] - shows technique but used as a Provisional Bind Off to hold stitches temporarily)

E-WRAP CAST ON:[29]
EW the peg and continue wrapping around the loom until there are 2 loops on every peg. Lift bottom loop over the top on all pegs; by lifting the bottom loop over this is called **Knitting Over** or **Working the stitch**. The yarn all gets knitted and falls inside the circle and comes out through the bottom. The front of the fabric, called the **Right Side**, shows on the outside of the loom. An E-wrap Cast On is a looser cast on with loopy edges.

TIGHT E-WRAP CAST ON:[30]
The first row of this cast on is the same as the E-wrap Cast On. For the second row use a Flat Knit stitch.

**DOUBLE STITCH (DS) CAST ON:**
The Double Stitch (DS) is a method that produces a less stretchy and dense (less gaps) than the e-wrap. It is good when using one strand of yarn when the space between the pegs (loom gauge) is too big.

Work the Double Stitch Cast On by e-wrapping all the pegs 3 times then knitting over bottom loop over top two loops.
If "knitting in the round" you will wrap the 3 rounds, around the loom, 3 full times.
If a flat panel: E-Wrap the row, turn to wrap a second row, then turn to wrap the third row. After casting on, only EW loom one time but lift bottom loop over top two.

**CHUNKY BRAID STITCH (CBS) CAST ON:**
The CHUNKY BRAID Stitch (CBS) is a method that looks like a knitted braid. The fabric is non-stretchy and tight.  This stitch works well with thin yarn on an Extra Large Gauge loom or to close gaps where the yarn seems too thin for the loom used.  To produce this stitch wrap the loom as if to use the DOUBLE STITCH (DS) and then wrap the loom one more time.  Knit three stitches over one.  The next round or row wrap the loom 3 more times and repeat.  This stitch is also called the 3 over 1 stitch.

## FLAT KNIT STITCH (FK):[31]

A type of knit stitch that lays flat and smooth; it has a classic knit v-shape.
The flat knit stitch is worked by laying the yarn above the existing loop on the peg and knitting over the bottom loop over the top. The stitch is named flat because it is held above the pegs flat instead of wrapping around the peg. It can be too tight for some knitters though.

*TIP: If you knit tight, after flat knitting a peg, tug on that loop before knitting the next peg. This will loosen more yarn into the stitch.*

## PURL (P):[32]

This stitch is opposite of a knit stitch and makes an outward bump on the fabric. Opposite means that when you make a knit stitch, the back or wrong side of the fabric actually is a purl bump. So when a purl is made, on the front or right side of the fabric, a knit stitch is on the wrong side.
• The purl stitch starts by laying the yarn below the existing loop on the peg.
• With your loom tool, place it above the loop and slide it under that loop, grab (or scoop) the working yarn through the loop to make a new loop. "Slide and scoop, pull up a loop"!
• With the loom tool hold the new loop and pull up so the old loop comes off the peg.
• Place the new loop on the peg, with the old loop now inside the loom, and gently pull the working yarn so the new loop is snug on the peg.

*TIP: Think of this as pulling up a pearl from the ocean.*

## GARTER STITCH PATTERN:[33]

Stitch pattern of Knit and Purl rows. Knit rows and purl rows repeat after each other; looks like a ridge. A Knit could be an E-wrap for a stretchy fabric or Flat Knit* for something more rigid. *There is also a U-Knit stitch or standard Knit stitch not covered here that can be used as well. The U-Knit and the Knit look the same. A "reverse purl" is how the Knit is made.

## DIAMOND LACE STITCH (DLS):[34]

A mesh looking fabric made from a series of working pairs of stitches, back and forth across a row or round, until all stitches are worked twice; the row or round usually appears twice the length as a one in a basic knit stitch would.
Starting with the working strand on the last peg; Skip the next peg and EW the peg after.

Now go back and wrap the first skipped peg.
Two pegs are wrapped. Knit over both pegs.
Repeat DLS until tube measures desired length.

## BASIC FLAT PANEL BIND OFF (also called Simple Bind Off):[35]
Working yarn will be on the last stitch worked and you'll be working back to take the knitting off the loom. Call this peg your peg 1 for directions below.
EW peg 1 (last stitch worked) and *EW peg 2. Pick up peg 2 loop and onto peg 1. Work stitch by lifting bottom over the top.
Pick up loop on peg 1 and move to peg 2. Peg 2 is now your new peg 1*.

Repeat the directions from * to * until 1 stitch remains.  EW the last stitch.  Cut yarn and pull tail through the loop. Weave in your tail.

> **TIP:** E-Wrap stitch will be looser. For a tighter bind off use a flat knit stitch
.

## HAT BRIMS (edge of hat):[36]
Hat brims can be rolled, hemmed or more tailored.  If a hat has only a knit type stitch (Example all EW) then the end of that hat will curl or roll. To keep the hat from rolling, and easy way is to make or "hang" a hemmed brim. Other brims are popular, too but require using the purl stitch (see **PURL**). Some of these are a garter stitch, rib or seed stitch pattern. Brims can be used on other projects as well.

## HEMMED BRIM:[37]
Knit double the length desired for brim or follow directions given in your pattern; make sure you are at the beginning of your round. Reach inside and pull up the beginning edge to the inside of the hat. Use the beginning tail to guide lining up the first stitch with the first peg. Pick up bottom loose loop and place on peg 1. Do this for all pegs. Check that the stitches are lined up then lift bottom loop over top to lock in the hem. Continue knitting in the round and working stitches as pattern calls.

## GATHERED or DRAWSTRING BIND-OFF (Cast-off):[38]
This gathered bind-off makes a drawstring in the ending loops of a tube of knitting; used mostly in simple hats.
1. With working the yarn wrap loom one and a half (1.5) times around circumference and cut yarn.
2. Use your tapestry needle and thread the long tail end into the needle.  Put needle through bottom of loop on peg 1. Pull all extra yarn through. Do this again through all loops on the loom to the right or same direction. When all loops have been threaded, pull through beginning peg one more time. Take all loops off the loom.

3. Turn inside out and pull gently on the drawstring to tighten. With the needle, put it through a close loop and pull but not all the way. Before pulling tight put needle through the new loop. Pull tight to make a knot. Sew through a few times to close hole and make another knot. Cut a 1" tail. This will be hidden. Turn hat right side out again.

## WEAVE:[39]

To use a tapestry needle with remaining tails and sew into the fabric to hide or finish off the project. The tails are usually from the remaining tails from cast on, bind offs or color changes. Place a tapestry needle (yarn needle) on the end of a tail. Work the tail through stitches on the wrong side of the work. Start with a stitch that is closest to the base of the tail and work through one stitch at a time going about half the length of the tail. Insert the needle through the "bump" of each stitch. Turn direction the opposite way and go back through those stitches again. If the yarn type allows, try to push the needle through the first part of your woven tail so it splits the yarn. Do this a few times until you run out of tail. This will lock the tail into place and not come out in the wash or during wear.

## WHIPSTITCH (SEW):[40]

The act of sewing together two panels, or ends of fabric, to connect. A whipstitch gets the name from whipping around the outside of two edges places front to front; this is also called a blanket stitch. (Video Link - Invisible Seam[41])

Place two right-sided fabrics together and line up edges. Insert tapestry needle from back panel to front panel through both edges and pull yarn through. (Run through both top loops of each edge). Repeat across all stitches on edge. Tie knot and weave in remaining yarn or trim with scissors.

## I-CORD:

I-cord is a knit cord made from a few stitches knit continually until the desired length is made; it is a narrow cording. I-cord is usually 2-4 stitches wide but can be larger and is used for embellishments, handles and ties.

Cast On desired number of stitches. Pass the working yarn to the inside of the loom, behind the cast on stitches, and back to the starting peg.
Hold the yarn flat above the loops and knit off each stitch.
Repeat these steps until desired length; you will see a tight tube forming.

To finish, move peg 2 to peg 1 and knit off. Move loop from peg 1 to peg 2 and repeat steps until one loop remains. Cut a 6-inch tail and pull through last loop and weave in tail(s) to center.

## SKILL LEVELS:

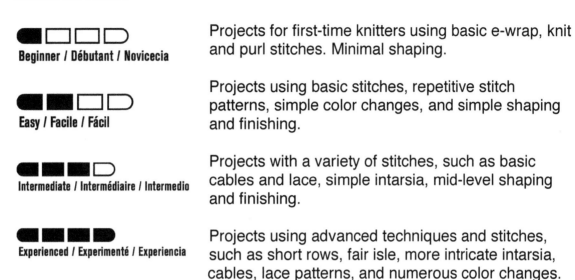

**Beginner / Débutant / Novicecia**

Projects for first-time knitters using basic e-wrap, knit and purl stitches. Minimal shaping.

**Easy / Facile / Fácil**

Projects using basic stitches, repetitive stitch patterns, simple color changes, and simple shaping and finishing.

**Intermediate / Intermédiaire / Intermedio**

Projects with a variety of stitches, such as basic cables and lace, simple intarsia, mid-level shaping and finishing.

**Experienced / Experimenté / Experiencia**

Projects using advanced techniques and stitches, such as short rows, fair isle, more intricate intarsia, cables, lace patterns, and numerous color changes.

# Stitches & Technique Video References and more!

### Casting On - CO = CAST-ON:
There are many different ways to get yarn on the loom to begin knitting and this is called Casting On.

In this edition you will find links to videos of Loom Knit Cast on Methods for the knitting loom.  Most are for single knit and some are double.  They are shown on a loom in a flat panel but can be connected to be used **IN THE ROUND** (or for "circular" knitting) for a hat, bag, tub scarf, etc. It doesn't matter what loom this occurs on; just make sure you use an appropriate yarn or number of strands for the gauge of that loom.

(***loom shown in the first set of links is Knitting Board AllnOne loom with 3/8" small gauge; again your loom could be a large gauge plastic loom and it will work the same, the stitches will just be larger with less "stitches per inch" (or cm).***)

**To see the video instructions listed, visit the website with the endnote number (or in eBook click the link).**

- Loom Knit Cast On Overview with swatches[42].
- E-wrap CO[43].
- Long Tail & Long Tail Ribbed CO[44].
- Half Hitch Cast On or Backwards loop[45].
- Yarn Over or Double E-wrap CO[46].
- True Cable CO (easy no crochet hook) matches needle version[47].
- Chain Cast On[48].
- Crochet Cast On[49].
- Scalloped Cast On[50].
- Cable Cast On (braided on right side)[51].
- Diamond Lace or Figure 8 Cast on Single Knitting[52].
- Adjustable CO[53].
- Classic Knit CO[54].
- Purl CO[55].
- Picot CO[56].
- Quick Half Hitch CO[57].
- Modified Drawstring CO[58].  or use the first version at
- How to Drawstring Cast on a round loom Loom Knit[59].
- S loom with crochet hook[60].
- Finish Cast on edge of scarf or panel[61].
- Roll Free Edge Rib Stitch for hat brim or blanket[62].
- Crochet Cast on Long Loom[63].
- Easy Chain CO with crochet hook[64].

**LOOM REFERENCES: LOOM VIDEO PLAYLISTS**
Here are a few more video playlist for reference.

Loom Stitches[65]
Casting On[66]
Bind off[67]
Videos on long loom[68]

## LOOM KNIT STITCHES

Below you will find loom knit stitches and loom knit stitch patterns with links to a video or article on how a stitch or stitch pattern is made.  Please keep in mind there are times that a needle stitch or stitch pattern calls out one name (of multiple names) and the loom name may not be the same.  Also there can be more than one name for the same stitch.  We have tried to reference multiple names for these stitches.  This is not meant to cause confusion but to help if you find a pattern and you are not familiar with the stitch.  Just visit our site to search for that stitch name and see if we have referenced it.  This list is **not** complete; please check our website or new editions for added information and reference.

## STITCHES

Easy Bobble or Popcorn Stitch[69].
P2tog or Purl 2 Together and YO or Yarn Over[70].
Double Knit 8 or EW or Twisted Knit[71].
Knit (k) Stitch[72].
Beginner E wrap (ew) Stitch now with CC[73].
Purl (p) Stitch[74].
Single Rib Stitch[75].
Twisted Knit Stitch[76].
Stitches side by side, Rib Stitches & Twisted Knit Stitch[77].

## STITCH PATTERNS

Decrease Figure 8 Stitch[78].
Increase Figure 8 Stitch[79].
Figure 8, Fishnet or Diamond Lace Stitch[80].
Hat Brim that doesn't roll Garter Stitch[81].
Seed Stitch[82].
Moss Stitch[83].
Crossed Stockinette (ew & k)[84].
Garter (k & p)[85].
Triple Knit Stitch[86].

**DONATING YOUR WORK**

Once you get started making your first hat or scarf it is natural to get excited and make several to donate or give away. That's fantastic! Many times giving is a pleasant experience but sometimes, in our excitement, we forget that there may be guidelines or restrictions a charity, hospital or even an individual may have such as a cancer patient or a newborn. These can range from a sensitivity to specific materials or the need for the item to be more stretchy.

The following article was published on the GoodKnit Kisses website to further explain. On the next page you will find smaller images of the checklist, worksheet and tax log you can download from the website for free. The direct link is also in our endnotes as well.

HOW TO MAKE DONATING HANDMADE A PLEASANT EXPERIENCE

Anyone who crochets or knits (with needles or loom) will make items for friends, colleagues, family and beyond. At some point you have already or plan on donating handmade to the less fortunate.

We, as crafters, donate to hospitals, homeless shelters, women shelters, men shelters and our local churches. I'm sure there are many more places as the list can go on with opportunities donating handmade goods.

We treasure the opportunity to do what we love and take pride in our work. Imagine yourself taking your gifts that you spent a lot of time and effort in making to an organization. Enthusiastically you tell the individual at reception you have items you made to donate.

The person in charge of receiving donated item meets you; takes a look at your precious gift and says, "None of these items are suitable for what we need." You leave heartbroken and feel that this may have been a waste of time.

Donating handmade items shouldn't be a sour experience. Here are some tips and free PDF downloads for donating handmade items!

Stasia Neal Renfrew (Blogger of Loom Knitting Central & a member of the GoodKnit Kisses Loom & Craft Club Facebook group) shared this information after having a conversation with a volunteer coordinator:

1. Use yarns accepted by the facility or group you are donating to, because of allergies and sensitivities that some babies and young children and adults have not all donations can be used.
2. Ask what is needed, some charities get overloaded with hats or afghans that don't get used and eventually end up donated to Salvation Army or other such organizations. Make sure you are creating something they can use and if they can't they might be able to point to another organization that can use what you have created.
3. Ask beforehand if you want a receipt for your donation; because asking at tax time they are more reluctant due to the possibility of fraud. (They have to protect themselves as well).

Donation Downloads

With this in mind we have created **three templates** that will assist in making your gift of giving a pleasant one. I recommend placing in a notebook or binder. Keep a record of the places you donate. Keep or print a clean copy for changes or new places to donate.

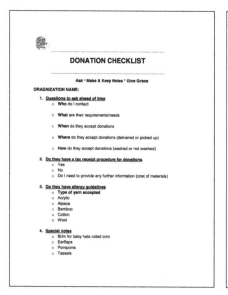
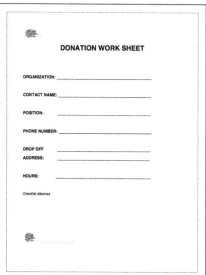

Donation Check List[87]: Use this check list to record necessary information for the Organization's donating guidelines.

Donation Worksheet[88]:
A place to record the Organization's contact information.

Donation Tax Log[89]: Keep track of what Organizations you donated items and noting if they provide tax receipts & do you receive one

# Chapter 2

**Overview Reading Patterns and Charts**:
The patterns here will have instructions written out. Many times rows are repeated but it saves space to tell you to repeat those rows again. To help show you what the project looks like there are charts sometimes in patterns. Charts also appear in needle patterns and are a great ways to convert to loom knitting, as all show graphically the "Right Side" or RS of the knitting like a loom knit project. For a full article on converting patterns without charts, from needle to loom, see **Converting Needle Patterns**.

Knitting charts are a graphic way to show what stitches are used. For every box on a chart it represents a stitch for your knitting. The charts always show one side (mostly the front or Right Side) of the knitting. Each symbol or even an empty box represents the type of stitch that is used or technique. A chart can be used for flat panel knitting or circular. (A double knitting pattern may have a chart but also a top view diagram of the loom. Double knitting will not be covered in this edition).

Flat panels work back and forth across the rows from right to left on the chart. For loom knitting and for needles "Row" numbers start on the right for all odd rows, even rows are on the left for working back in the other direction for flat panels. Knitting charts work from the bottom up because as you knit a row, the knitting falls below your pegs and you begin a new row. So read your chart starting at the bottom right and work to the left of the chart. When starting the next row on a project, worked "**in the round**", go back to the right of the chart to start the next row stitch. Again, when you make a **flat panel** (going back and forth; from left to right and then right to left repeating) you will end a row on the left of the chart and start the 1st stitch above that on the left for the next row.

| Key | |
|---|---|
| Cable 4 Back c4b | (RS) Sl 2 to back, k2, k2 sts from cn (WS) Sl 2 to front, p2, p2 sts from cn |
| Cable 4 Front c4f | (RS) Sl 2 to front, k2, k 2 sts from cn (WS) Sl 2 to back, p2, p 2 sts from cn |
| Knit k | (RS) Knit (WS) Purl |
| Purl p | (RS) Purl (WS) Knit |

**Chart Key:**
Before we start, here is a Chart Key. The Key shows the stitch names and corresponding symbol. Notice the RS (Right Side) stitch is noted. The WS (Wrong Side) is not pictured on the chart for loom or needle patterns. However, WS is noted for needles because that is the opposite stitch needed on the WS for flat panels to match the RS chart symbols/ stitches. Loom knitters can read a CHART and knit it as shown. Warning for Loom Knitters. If you convert a needle pattern that has a chart and written directions, you must ignore the WS rows as written and make them as shown on the chart. For more details on that see **Converting Needle Patterns**.

# Flat Knitting Chart:

The following is a simple pattern using knits and purl stitches. Study the chart before looking at the written pattern to check your work.

---

 **TIP:** Remember that your first stitch starts on the bottom row on the very first stitch to the right. This pattern is to be worked as a flat panel.

---

## Written Version:

Here is the pattern written out by stitch for the chart as seen for a LOOM.

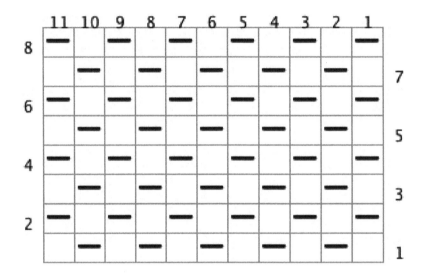

Row 1: K1, P1, K1, P1, K1, P1, K1, P1, K1, P1, K1
Row 2: P1, K1, P1, K1, P1, K1, P1, K1, P1, K1, P1
Row 3: K1, P1, K1, P1, K1, P1, K1, P1, K1, P1, K1
Row 4: P1, K1, P1, K1, P1, K1, P1, K1, P1, K1, P1
Row 5: K1, P1, K1, P1, K1, P1, K1, P1, K1, P1, K1
Row 6: P1, K1, P1, K1, P1, K1, P1, K1, P1, K1, P1
Row 7: K1, P1, K1, P1, K1, P1, K1, P1, K1, P1, K1
Row 8: P1, K1, P1, K1, P1, K1, P1, K1, P1, K1, P1

| Key | |
|-----|-----|
| ☐ | Knit k |
| (RS) Knit | |
| ▬ | Purl p |
| (RS) Purl | |

## Rows:

Notice how there are an even number of rows? This is because this stitch pattern is a "2 row repeat". It needs an even number of rows. Repeating rows 1 and 2 of this pattern will continue the design until stops by bind-off or another stitch pattern. Technically you can add 1 more row to make both ends of the pattern to look mirrored or "even" but isn't necessary for most patterns with this stitch. Always read all pattern notes on any pattern to make sure.

**Columns:**
Notice there is an odd number of columns? That is because the pattern is a "2 + 1". The stitch pattern needs a multiple of 2 stitches to repeat correctly for your pattern. If you were to continue the stitch pattern in the most stitches (on pegs or on needles) the amount cast on would need to be divisible by two. If we were knitting in the round, the pattern would simply repeat infinitely until ended for another stitch pattern or binding off.

For a flat panel, in order for the stitch pattern to look even on both edges of the pattern, an extra stitch must be added. For example: if a stitch pattern were a 6 + 1 you would need a multiple of 6 stitches plus 1 extra. i.e. 37 stitches for a larger project. 36 is divisible by 6 and 1 is added to make 37 total. See chart in **Circular Knitting** chart.

**Written Variations:**
When writing patterns many times they are shortened or condensed to save space. But these shortened ways also happen to easier to remember to chant in our brain! This works well with popular basic stitch patterns as will knit and purl combination patterns.

Here are some variations. To start, this is one way how this stitch pattern would be called out in a Stitch Book.

## VARIATION 1 (Simple Version):
**Seed Stitch**
*2 + 1*
*2 row rep (it may or may not say this)*

**Row 1 (RS)** *K1, *p1, k1; rep from * to end.*

That is the simplest way to write it is seen above.

**Did you see the asterisks?** Asterisks (*) are commonly used to identify a starting point for a repeat and the next asterisk is the end repeat for that area on that row.  You could have another set of asterisks or more later on in a row so paying attention to where they start and stop is important. Another way to write this repeating direction could be "repeat between *,*". I do that with my own patterns many times. Ex. To abbreviate more would read, "rep bet *, *".

 **GENERAL CHART TIPS: Use colors to help!**

*If you are visually minded, use book highlighters or colored pencils for different sections.*

*If you have a set of instructions between asterisks, and there are the same instructions down the row, then color it the same color.*

*If there is more than one set of instructions be sure to use different colors. You can even write yourself a color key on your printed page.*

*If you don't want to mark your book or page try laminating the page or in a plastic sheet or sleeve and use dry erase markers.*

*Charts can also be colored for difficult stitches.  Highlighting cables is an excellent use of color.*

*You can cross-reference this on a written pattern as well as the chart!*

## VARIATION 2 (Needle version):
**Seed Stitch**
*2 + 1*
*2-row rep*

**Row 1 (RS)** *K1, *p1, k1; rep from * to end.*
**Row 2 (WS)** *K1, *p1, k1; rep from * to end.*

NOTE that ROW 2 looks different than the chart? This Version is written as for needles.  A loom version would be written already converted. See **Converting Needle Patterns**.

For a chart with needles the Key may actually state on WS rows to purl the knit symbol and knit the purl symbol for even rows OR odd rows, whichever in that pattern is the wring side or WS. A loom Key doesn't have to call that out.

## VARIATION 3 (Loom version):
**Seed Stitch**
*2 + 1*
*2-row rep*

**Row 1** *K1, \*p1, k1; rep from \* to end.*
**Row 2** *P1, \*k1, p1; rep from \* to end.*


## VARIATION 4 (Loom version - LONG):
**Seed Stitch**
*2 + 1*
*2 row rep*

**Row 1** K1, P1, K1, P1, K1, P1, K1, P1, K1, P1, K1
**Row 2** P1, K1, P1, K1, P1, K1, P1, K1, P1, K1, P1
**Row 3** K1, P1, K1, P1, K1, P1, K1, P1, K1, P1, K1
**Row 4** P1, K1, P1, K1, P1, K1, P1, K1, P1, K1, P1
**Row 5** K1, P1, K1, P1, K1, P1, K1, P1, K1, P1, K1
**Row 6** P1, K1, P1, K1, P1, K1, P1, K1, P1, K1, P1
**Row 7** K1, P1, K1, P1, K1, P1, K1, P1, K1, P1, K1
**Row 8** P1, K1, P1, K1, P1, K1, P1, K1, P1, K1, P1


**Consistency in Pattern Writing:**
Notice the Rows are written slightly different than I did before?  The rows are nearly identical as first written but one thing changed; it is a publishing/writing choice. Do you see it? It is "Row 1:" versus "**Row 1**". The first has a colon to separate the instructions from the row #.  The second has the row # bolded and then the instructions written without bolding. Both are acceptable.  The designer or publisher may choose whatever they like but will use the same style throughout a publication unless intentionally teaching differences in patter writing. Their format could change in another publication but it has no bearing on what is right or wrong. Consistency is King. This is just some food for thought when reading various written patterns. Pattern makers do make mistakes though.  If you come across something that appears to be a mistake be sure to visit their site or forums to check.  There may be a note about a revision.  If not you can also write the maker for clarification; they are usually happy to fix and/or explain.

## VARIATION 5 (Circular or "in-the-round"):
### Seed Stitch
*2 (+ 1)*
*2-row rep*

**Round 1** *\*K1, p1\*; rep from \* to end.*
**Round 2** *\*P1, k1\*; rep from \* to end.*

*Notice the +1 dropped? Look again at the asterisks. No +"any number" is needed for knitting in the round. The asterisks moved to the left and the extra k1 dropped from round 1 (and the last p1 dropped from round 2). The **extra stitch must go away** or when the row repeats itself the stitch pattern would have two same stitches in a round; which would be an error in the pattern.*

*Notice "Rows" changed to "Rounds"? When knitting around a loom in a circle, the rows usually are noted as rounds. Sometimes that word is overlooked, in new pattern writers directions, but it is a handy feature. Say you are working on a hat with a soft visor. The pattern may start calling out "Rows" and working as a flat panel; going back and forth from left to right and right to left. The pattern then changes to cast on the remaining stitches and join in the round. Now the pattern rows become written as "Rounds". It is easy to see how many rounds you have knitted. \*If you see the word row it is still not wrong as it is still expressed as a row when talking about gauge or just the lengthwise part of a knitted item; "round" is specific to knitting circular.*

### HOT TIP!
*For some patterns, like this one, if the pattern shifts by 1 stitch on each row then using an odd peg circular loom can make some 2 + 1 (and 2 row repeat) patterns super easy to convert from rows to rounds. For the pattern above you will simply continue to work the first round with the +1. because of the extra peg the pattern will continue to alternate. In fact if the peg count, less your +1 peg, is divisible by your multiplier then it can still work; you just need to study the pattern first. [For example a 6 + 1 (2 row repeat) stitch pattern would work for a 31-peg loom because 30 is divisible by 6 plus the extra 1 stitch. Just continue to work your Row 1 to include the plus 1 for a 1-row repeat on the pattern listed above. Not all will work out this way and this is why you will want to study a pattern before knitting up a sample/swatch.] (Reminder note: A circular loom can also be any round, oval or even a rectangular loom that knits circular).*

## Circular Knitting Chart:

The following is a simple pattern using knits and purl stitches again but for knitting "in-the-round". Study the chart before looking at the written pattern to check your work. TIP: Remember that your first stitch starts on the bottom round/ row on the very first stitch to the right.

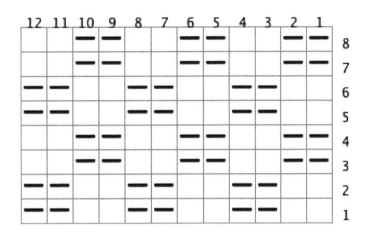

## Written Version:

Here is the pattern written out by stitch for the chart as seen for a LOOM.

Round 1: K2, P2, K2, P2, K2, P2, K2, P2, K2, P2
Round 2: P2, K2, P2, K2, P2, K2, P2, K2, P2, K2
Round 3: K2, P2, K2, P2, K2, P2, K2, P2, K2, P2
Round 4: P2, K2, P2, K2, P2, K2, P2, K2, P2, K2
Round 5: K2, P2, K2, P2, K2, P2, K2, P2, K2, P2
Round 6: P2, K2, P2, K2, P2, K2, P2, K2, P2, K2
Round 7: K2, P2, K2, P2, K2, P2, K2, P2, K2, P2
Round 8: P2, K2, P2, K2, P2, K2, P2, K2, P2, K2
*and the pattern continues....*

## Rows/Rounds:

Notice how there an even number of rows/rounds? This is because this stitch pattern is a "4 row repeat". It needs an even number of rows. Repeating rows 1-4 of this pattern will continue the design until stops by bind-off or another stitch pattern. In this pattern, similar to before, you can add 2 more rows to make both ends of the pattern to look mirrored or "even" but isn't necessary for most patterns with this stitch. Always read all pattern notes on any pattern to make sure.

## Columns:

Notice there is an even number of columns? That is because the pattern is circular and it works out that the next stitch on the next round will continue the pattern repeat correctly. The stitch pattern needs a multiple of 4 stitches to repeat correctly for the pattern. If you were to continue the stitch pattern in the most stitches (on pegs or on needles) the amount cast on would need to be divisible by four for this pattern. If we were knitting in the round, the pattern would simply repeat infinitely until ended for another stitch pattern or binding off.

For example: 36 stitches are divisible by a multiple of 4. This pattern would make a nice hat on a popular standardized Large Gauge loom; several manufacturers currently have their own version like this. An example of this hat is included in this book. Alternate looms are named in the pattern; it is good practice to try the same pattern on different looms. See **Bulky Moss Stitch** pattern.

Let's compare how this chart is written out in different variations as done with the flat knitting variations.

## VARIATION 1 Circular (Simple - Loom or Needle):
**Double Moss Stitch**
*Multiple of 4*
*4-row repeat*

**Rounds 1-2** *K1, k1*; rep from * to end.
**Rounds 3-4** *P1, p1*; rep from * to end.

That is the simplest way to write that stitch pattern. Notice how it is similar to Variation 5 in the flat knitting versions? The differences here are:
1.  The word "Multiple" is used to call out that the pattern stitch repeat is 4 instead of a number plus another number. This is yet another way it can be written.
2.  The word rep is now written as repeat and not abbreviated as well.
3.  Rounds 1-2 and 3-4 are combined together instead of written separate. This is because they do the same thing and therefore don't need to be written out in long form. A benefit of writing a pattern in long form would be the ability to cover up lines of rows or rounds already knit (or covering ones about to be knit.

*TIP: Use a large sticky note upside-down to cover up the part of a chart or written pattern you have not worked yet. When you come back to your knitting you'll know where you finished. When you are ready to start the next row simply uncover only the next row.*

## VARIATION 2 Circular (Loom or Needle):
### *Double Moss Stitch*

*Cast on 36 stitches*

**Round 1** *\*K1, k1\*; rep from \* to end.*
**Round 2** *\*K1, k1\*; rep from \* to end.*
**Round 3** *\*P1, p1\*; rep from \* to end.*
**Round 4** *\*P1, p1\*; rep from \* to end.*
*Repeat Rounds 1-4 until desired length.*

This version simply spells out all four rounds and adds a note to repeat the rounds 4 times; this is instead of calling it out in the beginning. It also doesn't state the multiple but explains how many stitches to cast-on. This type of variation is typical for patterns as the other variations are more typical for "stitch patterns" which are often used to build patterns.

**Wrapping up! – Keys to Pattern Reading**
The variations on pattern writing are infinite as there are unique individual writing them.  The keys to reading patterns are:
• Read the pattern through once.
• Study the parts of the pattern that give you trouble.
• Make notes if needed on the pattern.
• Read through the pattern again mentally making the stitches as you go.
• Check the book or pattern for terms or explanations found elsewhere.
• Make a swatch! Go ahead and make a swatch in the yarn and loom you intend to use before going further to ask for help.  Test out what you just read first and will be surprised what you can do.  It will also help when getting help from someone else if you have already attempted the stitch or technique.
• If you continue to not understand part of a pattern consult other books, resources, websites and forums.
• The pattern writer or designer may or may not be available but they are a great place to contact for the pattern; especially if it is a current self-published pattern on the yarn community site Ravelry.com or similar. Be sure you have really familiarized yourself with the pattern before contacting a designer as a best practice.

More tips/answers are:
• 	*Yes, you CAN do this!* Repeat from *,*.
• 	Yes, you CAN change the yarn color or thickness; by all means make it your own.  This is the fun stuff!
• 	Yes, it WILL change the stitch count if the yarn is a different weight; check article on **Why Swatch**. And yes, you will likely have to change the stitch count for that.
• 	Yes, you can change the size for many patterns.  No, it doesn't make the pattern a "new" pattern. You will likely need to study the pattern, make a small swatch and do a little math. Don't worry, we have math in this book for that! See **Knitter's Math and Size Charts** chapter 5.

Now that you have tried two simple patterns you are ready to look at one that is a little more difficult. It is still a Basic pattern category, not Easy or Beginner, but it is only still knits and purls. Try walking through the pattern below and Knit up a swatch on your favorite loom.


**Your Homework Assignment starts on the next page! You can do this!**

Homework:

## PYRAMID STITCH

This Pyramid Stitch pattern is written for flat and circular knitting. Please read all notes. Omit column 1 for circular knitting or see circular chart. The pyramid stitch pattern is a multiple of 8 +1 and a 16-row repeat. Chart and rows are written using 24 stitches wide (3 stitch repeats) + 1 and 32 rows (2-row repeats). Pattern is written for a main stitch pattern and may or may not require a border depending on the item being made. For an item requiring a border, allow cast on and border of your choice in style and width plus bind off. For swatch homework purposes merely cast-on and start knitting. When finished bind-off. See **Glossary** for stitches and terms.

[For a garter stitch border allow minimum 8 extra stitches, 4 on left and 4 on right, and 6-8 rows on each end for garter stitch rows; for example if on a blanket. To make a hat, a 1×1 ribbing would look nice with the pyramid stitch pattern.]

### _Video[90]_ _references for stitches (click on hyperlinks):_
Stitches:
Knit[91] (use U-Knit or True Knit/Reverse purl) – note: E-wrap can be used but will create a more stretchy Y-shaped stitch that is twisted and larger than a smooth V-shaped Knit stitch. Your fabric will be more stretchy, larger and bumpier than a U or regular knit.
Purl[92]

## Looms and Yarn Choice:
Use a loom in your collection that has the required about of pegs you can knit the panel on. If you are knitting in the round pick a loom that has the exact number of pegs in the pattern. If you have a loom that is adjustable in size (meaning you can change the peg count) then use that if the exact number of pegs can be chosen.

After choosing your loom, choose an appropriate weight (size) yarn. As your collection and learning grows you will find your will start to choose your yarn first and then find the appropriate loom. For practice just grab a loom and yarn. For yarn weight suggestions for YOUR loom see our handy **Loom Gauge Chart** with all the information at your fingertips.

## Pyramid Stitch Pattern
Instructions for <u>Flat Panel Knitting</u>

Cast on 25 stitches.
(Cast on a multiple of 8 sts + 1 and a 16-row repeat; CHART & ROWS Show 3 Stitch Patterns wide and 2 row pattern repeats).

Row 1: p1, k7, p1, k7, p1, k7, p1
Row 2: p1, k7, p1, k7, p1, k7, p1
Row 3: p2, k5, p3, k5, p3, k5, p2
Row 4: p2, k5, p3, k5, p3, k5, p2
Row 5: p3, k3, p5, k3, p5, k3, p3
Row 6: p3, k3, p5, k3, p5, k3, p3
Row 7: p4, k1, p7, k1, p7, k1, p4
Row 8: p4, k1, p7, k1, p7, k1, p4
Row 9: k4, p1, k7, p1, k7, p1, k4
Row 10: k4, p1, k7, p1, k7, p1, k4
Row 11: k3, p3, k5, p3, k5, p3, k3
Row 12: k3, p3, k5, p3, k5, p3, k3
Row 13: k2, p5, k3, p5, k3, p5, k2
Row 14: k2, p5, k3, p5, k3, p5, k2
Row 15: k1, p7, k1, p7, k1, p7, k1
Row 16: k1, p7, k1, p7, k1, p7, k1
Row 17: p1, k7, p1, k7, p1, k7, p1
Row 18: p1, k7, p1, k7, p1, k7, p1
Row 19: p2, k5, p3, k5, p3, k5, p2
Row 20: p2, k5, p3, k5, p3, k5, p2
Row 21: p3, k3, p5, k3, p5, k3, p3
Row 22: p3, k3, p5, k3, p5, k3, p3
Row 23: p4, k1, p7, k1, p7, k1, p4
Row 24: p4, k1, p7, k1, p7, k1, p4
Row 25: k4, p1, k7, p1, k7, p1, k4
Row 26: k4, p1, k7, p1, k7, p1, k4
Row 27: k3, p3, k5, p3, k5, p3, k3
Row 28: k3, p3, k5, p3, k5, p3, k3
Row 29: k2, p5, k3, p5, k3, p5, k2
Row 30: k2, p5, k3, p5, k3, p5, k2
Row 31: k1, p7, k1, p7, k1, p7, k1
Row 32: k1, p7, k1, p7, k1, p7, k1

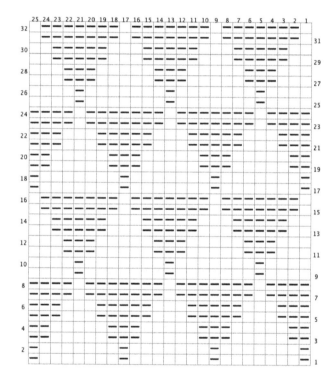

Key

☐ Knit
k
(RS) Knit

▬ Purl
p
(RS) Purl

**Pyramid Stitch Pattern**
Instructions for <u>Circular Knitting</u>

Cast on 24 stitches.

(Cast on a multiple of 8 sts and a 16-row repeat; CHART & ROWS Show 3 Stitch Patterns wide and 2 row pattern repeats).

Round 1: k7, p1, k7, p1, k7, p1
Round 2: k7, p1, k7, p1, k7, p1
Round 3: k5, p3, k5, p3, k5, p2
Round 4: k5, p3, k5, p3, k5, p2
Round 5: k3, p5, k3, p5, k3, p3
Round 6: k3, p5, k3, p5, k3, p3
Round 7: k1, p7, k1, p7, k1, p4
Round 8: k1, p7, k1, p7, k1, p4
Round 9: p1, k7, p1, k7, p1, k4
Round 10: p1, k7, p1, k7, p1, k4
Round 11: p3, k5, p3, k5, p3, k3
Round 12: p3, k5, p3, k5, p3, k3
Round 13: p5, k3, p5, k3, p5, k2
Round 14: p5, k3, p5, k3, p5, k2
Round 15: p7, k1, p7, k1, p7, k1
Round 16: p7, k1, p7, k1, p7, k1
Round 17: k7, p1, k7, p1, k7, p1
Round 18: k7, p1, k7, p1, k7, p1
Round 19: k5, p3, k5, p3, k5, p2
Round 20: k5, p3, k5, p3, k5, p2
Round 21: k3, p5, k3, p5, k3, p3
Round 22: k3, p5, k3, p5, k3, p3
Round 23: k1, p7, k1, p7, k1, p4
Round 24: k1, p7, k1, p7, k1, p4
Round 25: p1, k7, p1, k7, p1, k4
Round 26: p1, k7, p1, k7, p1, k4
Round 27: p3, k5, p3, k5, p3, k3
Round 28: p3, k5, p3, k5, p3, k3
Round 29: p5, k3, p5, k3, p5, k2
Round 30: p5, k3, p5, k3, p5, k2
Round 31: p7, k1, p7, k1, p7, k1
Round 32: p7, k1, p7, k1, p7, k1

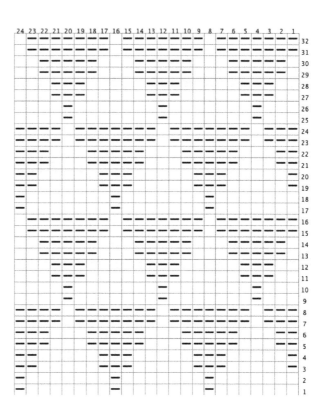

Bind off knitting or swatch. Way to go, you did it!

2nd Homework Assignment: Use blocking instructions. **Block** your swatch or larger knitting sample; then measure to check your **Knitting Gauge**.

## Converting Needle Patterns

The task of converting knitting patterns to loom can seem scary but the rewards are a treasure trove of beautiful knits by inspiring knitters of old and new!

There are hundreds of loom patterns on Ravelry. To date 1,500+ loom knit patterns can be found on Ravelry.com alone. However, there are thousands more needle and stitch patterns waiting to be discovered by loom knitters. This makes converting knitting patterns to loom necessary, should you wish to dive into a pattern originally made on needles. You can do this. All it takes is some time and patience…and maybe some notes and caffeine wouldn't hurt!

Loom knitting is always knit on the Right Ride (RS) of the fabric. The right side is always facing toward you or the front of the loom.

Needle knitters must turn their needles to the opposite side (Wrong Side) and work backwards with the opposite stitch they want shown on the front or RS.
- For needles in a flat panel (single knitting), the wrong side (WS) rows need to be converted.
- For circular knitting, also known as knitting in the round, both are always the RS unless there is some flat panel shaping involved.

## Stitch Conversion Chart – Convert WS stitches to RS

I suggest becoming comfortable with basic stitches and small decreases. Here is a list of basic stitches to learn before converting:

- Know the difference: U-knit, flat knit and reverse purl [true knit] versus an e-wrap which is a twisted stitch or k1tbl (knit 1 through the pack loop) – in needle patterns you'll mostly use a U-knit or true knit when the pattern says "knit" or "work stockinette"
- Purl & and the twisted version: ptbl or purl though the back loop. The ptbl is rarely used but is a stretchy & twisted purl stitch. Flip the new loop to twist like an e-wrap before putting on peg again).
- slip (a skipped stitch that can be at the beginning of the row or anywhere before the last stitch of the row).
- wyif & wyib (a slipped stitch – with yarn in front or with yarn in back)
- k2tog & ssk (mirrored knit decreases – k2tog leans right & ssk leans left).
- p2tog & ssp (mirrored purl decreases – p2tog leans right & ssk leans left).

*Quick Rule of Thumb: If knitting in the round, use all the same stitches as a needle pattern, for a flat panel use the opposite stitch for WS (Wrong side) if written out. If the needle pattern has a chart simply knit as the chart says starting from the bottom and working upward.* Stitches on the WS will need to become the opposite stitch or lean an opposite direction when converting knitting patterns to loom.

For example: A knit will become a purl and a purl becomes a knit.

## Stitch Conversion: Equivalents

| Wrong-sided (WS) | Right-Sided (RS) |
|---|---|
| | |
| **Basic Stitches** | |
| P (purl) | K (knit) |
| K (knit) | P (purl) |
| P tbl (purl in back) | K tbl (knit in back) |
| K tbl (purl in back) | P tbl (knit in back) |
| Sl wyif | Sl wyib |
| Sl wyib | Sl wyif |
| | |
| **Cable/Cross/Twist Stitches** | |
| Cross L, Knit | Cross R, Purled |
| Cross R, Purled | Cross L, Knit |
| Cross R, Knit | Cross L, Purled |
| Cross L, Purled | Cross R, Knit |
| Cable Stitches | |
| cX over Y left, knit* | cY over X left, purl* |
| cX over Y left, purl* | cY over X left, knit* |
| cX over Y right, knit* | cY over X right, purl* |
| cX over Y right, purl* | cY over X right, knit* |
| | |
| **Decreases** | |
| P2tog | K2tog |
| P2tog tbl | Sl1 K1 psso or work ssk |
| K2tog | P2tog |
| K2tog tbl | P2tog tbl |
| P3tog | K3tog |
| K3tog | P3tog |
| P2tog pnso | Sl1 K2tog psso |
| Sl1 K2tog psso | P2tog pnso |
| | |
| **Increases** | |
| P into back and front | K into front and back |
| P into front and back | K into back and front |
| K into back and front | P into front and back |
| K into front and back | P into back and front |

*Handy chart for converting stitches to the "opposite" stitch for the WS for loom knitting. Also handy for converting a flat piece of needle knitting into circular.

## Guidelines and Tips

**Loom size vs. needles size:**
Converting knitting patterns to loom also requires figuring out which loom gauge to use. For a chart with common looms and needle size equivalents see Chapter 4 on **Gauge**.

**Charts:**
Read previous notes above on understanding knitting charts.

**To help you get started there are some simple guidelines to make converting knitting patterns to loom simpler:**
NOTE: Needle patterns usually need the FIRST ROW directionally headed clockwise (right to left). _ 9 8 7 6 5 4 3 2 1,
>    1. To get the pattern in the right order you'll need to START your cast on from left to right (counterclockwise) in a cast on type that will cast on in the first pass (best cast on type listed below**) _ 1 2 3 4 5 6 7 8 9.
>    2. For Row 1 simply change direction and knit row. If it states RS knit as usual. If it states WS you will need to convert the stitches to the opposite stitch as shown below in the handy chart.

*Many times the even numbered rows are WS (Wrong Side). Be sure to read **all** notes in the entire pattern before converting. There may be key information you need to make the best choices.

## Best Cast-On Types

The best cast-on types are listed below for converting from needle to loom; use the endnotes in the book and links for eBook.
Long Tail & Long Tail Ribbed CO[93] –
Matches Longtail cast on.
Half Hitch Cast On or Backwards loop[94] –
Matches a "Thumb" cast on.
Loom Knit Cast On: Yarn Over or Double E-wrap[95] –
a loose cast on for converting knitting patterns to loom that need non-firm edge.
True Cable Cast On[96] – Matches Cable Cast on.
Chain Cast On[97]
Crochet Cast On[98]
Classic Knit Cast On[99] – Matches Knit Cast on.
Purl Cast On[100] – Matches a Purl Cast on.
Picot Cast On[101] – close match to a picot cast on, multiples may need adjusting.

# Chapter 3

Below you will find links to videos for Loom Knit techniques from various videos. Be sure to read the whole title to find the right technique for you. Many of my videos have extra tips that apply from time-to-time for troubleshooting.

## Earflaps on Hats/ Beanies

Many people love the look of earflaps for photo props, for fashion or simply to keep ears warm. Learn how to calculate that formula and apply it to the loom you need. To begin, you'll need a loom that is round or knits circular and appropriate yarn for that loom. After this you'll need to decide if you want the earflaps to be a rectangle or more of a triangular shape that slowly increases.

**Earflap Formula (Math)** – Fit for any size head

**Front of Hat** – Total pegs div by 3 = Front
* Explained: Count your pegs and divide the total number of pegs by 3; round up to the next whole number. This number will be the front of the hat and the pegs will stay empty while making the earflaps.

**Back of Hat** – Rem. number pegs div by 3 = Back
* Explained: Take the remaining pegs, after the Front is taken out, and divide by 3. This 1/3 number will leave empty in the back (opposite of front).

**Earflaps** – Remaining 1/3 number
* Explained: The same number used for the back of the hat is the same number used for each earflap. This is the widest part of the earflap. An earflap can start and finish as the same width or start at a 1-3 stitches and gradually get wider. The widest point is this number.
* Sometimes the 1/3 number does not divide even. If this is the case, round up to the nearest whole number. This number will be each earflap width. The remaining peg number will now be the **Back of the Hat**.

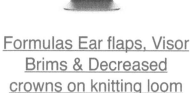

Formulas Ear flaps, Visor Brims & Decreased crowns on knitting loom

Earflap Talk on Knitting Loom: 24 peg blue circle loom Knifty Knitter

102                     103

**Directions to Knit Earflaps**

Now that you know your formula, mark your loom pegs with stitch markers according to the numbers above. Cast on the 1st earflap and increase on the ends every other row until it is to the desired width and length. Cut a long tail and knit the 2nd earflap. After the 2nd earflap continue knitting the row, cast on the empty pegs between the 1st earflap and knit the row above the 1st earflap. Continue on and cast on the remaining empty pegs until you reach the 2nd earflap. Mark the next peg as the beginning of your row. Start knitting your hat design.

104                    105

Loom Knit:            Increase by 1 - Half
Increase by 2          Stitch or Cleaner

Loom Knit: Half Stitch
technique or Cleaner
garter edge on purl rows

106

## Visors on Hats/ Beanies – Soft Brim

Newsboy hats with visors are always a classic feature for a hat that can be made easily.  Learn how to calculate the formula and apply it to the loom you need. To begin, you'll need a loom that is round or knits circular and appropriate yarn for that loom.

**Visor Formula (Math)** – Fit for any size head

**Front Edge of Visor** – Total pegs div by 3 = Front End (start)
- Explained: Count your pegs and divide the total number of pegs by 3; round up to the next whole number.  This number will be the front of the hat. Cast on this number of pegs. **TIP:** Use a starter peg to start your slipknot. A hard or bulky slipknot in the edge of your visor doesn't look or feel nice. If your loom doesn't have a starter peg, try a peg further away. After knitting a few rows you can take it off and the slipknot will pull right out.

**Visor Width** – Total pegs div by 2 = Visor Width (end)
- Explained: The widest point of the visor is this number. The visor gets cast on and then increases evenly on each side until it reaches this width.

## Directions to Knit Visors

Now that you know your formula, mark your loom pegs with stitch markers according to the numbers above. Cast on the Front Edge number and increase on the ends every other row until it is to the desired Visor Width; the width is half your peg count. Continue on and cast on the remaining empty pegs until all pegs are casted on.  Mark the next peg as the beginning of your row. Start knitting your hat design.

**TIP:** Start by knitting a brim that will not curl. Alternate knits and purls.

# Hat Crown Solutions

Options for decreasing the bulkiness of a hat crown:
- Modified Gathered Bind off
- Flat Drawstring Bind Off
- Decreased Crown (varies)
- Wedges

My favorite new method for a decreased crown is the Modified Gathered Bind off. This method I developed to lessen the need to use math to decrease and move a bunch of stitches around. I've written a detailed explanation below. Video Links to other techniques are also found below.

The Modified Gathered Bind Off is meant to be an alternative to a regular gathered bind off, which can create a bulky top. The Decreased Drown method causes problems in some yarns or some looms may also experience gaps. This modified method will create about two rows worth of knitting and be much flatter or totally flat versus other methods. However, if your pattern uses a purl stitch: if you are working a garter stitch, ribbed stitch, or seed stitch there are directions in the Set-up section below to adapt stitch for pattern.

**Modified Gathered Bind off**

**Instructions:**
Use with any loom. If the loom has an odd number of pegs do not move over the stitch on the last peg.

**Set-up:**
When you're ready to finish the hat and bind off, move every other stitch over one peg. (Ex. move all even pegs to odd. Leave last loop alone if you are using an odd number of pegs).

Work the peg by lifting the bottom loop over-the-top loop to create a knit stitch. Or create a purl stitch by pulling the bottom loop through the top loop. (TIP: move stitches over while working last round before following steps below so the stitches are loose enough to move easily.)

**ROUND 1:**

**Step 1:**
Wrap working yarn around entire loom circumference one and a half times and cut yarn.
**Step 2:**
Using knitting tool, place yarn below the first peg with a loop, and pull all the way through as if to purl. Pull all working yarn through the loop and take loop off peg.

**Step 3:**
Passing the working yarn behind the pegs, skip the next peg holding a loop and move to the second peg with a loop. Repeat step 2.

Repeat Step 3 until 1 full round of knitting is off the loom (meaning you passed your staring point for that round/row.). It's important not to fully tighten or pull the slack just yet.

Note for odd # pegs: Treat last peg as "peg #1" on ROUND 2 (Begin pulling the yarn through from above with that peg, which on your loom might have ended up as one of 2 adjacent pegs with a loop remaining on each after Step 1).

**ROUND 2:**

**Step 4:**
Place yarn above first peg, with a loop, and pull all the way through as if to Reverse Purl (aka Knit). Pull all working yarn through the loop and take loop off peg.

**Step 5:**
Pass the working yarn behind the empty pegs and repeat Step 4 for the remaining loops on the loom. Continue until all stitches are off the loom.

Turn knitting inside out and gently start pulling on the working yarn to tighten the last two rounds of modified gathered bind off.

Tie a knot and weave in ends or cut.

**DECREASED CROWN OPTIONS (via Video links)**
- Modified Gathered Bind off[107].
- GoodKnitKisses Vlog talk on decrease crowns[108].
- Infant Hat Loom Decrease Crown 24 Peg Round Loom[109].
- Youth Hat Loom Decrease Crown 30 or 31 Peg Round Loom[110].
- Adult Hat Loom Decrease Crown 36 Peg Round Loom[111].

If you are decreasing a hat or item sometimes you may need to move it from a larger loom to another for an extremely flat crown, like a top hat.  Watch how to do this with this two part series.
PART 1 Decrease Crown 48 Peg Round Purple Knifty Knitter loom sm gauge Adult[112].
PART 2 Transfer 48 peg Decrease Crown to 24 peg Round Knifty Knitter Loom[113].

# Tutorial References for Techniques

In future editions this area will expand. For now I wanted to include some reference videos on techniques I have featured.  Many of them are tried and true techniques and tips and some are just ways I have found I like to do things personally.  Personally I learn and grow in my own techniques over time just as you do.  Please know that there are no hard and fast rules of knitting since there are countless ways to get the same look or have a well made and finished piece. There could be better ways or ones that I improve on after showcasing a technique.  Please take this list and things in this book at face value and above all, have FUN with your knitting!

## CHANGE COLOR

Do you need to change colors or balls of yarn on the loom?  There are many techniques.

1. **KNOT** - Tie in the change with a knot is the most secure way but it does leave a knot.  I try to hide this part. The downside is you will have to weave in the tails later.
2. **DOUBLED UP** - Another way is to hide in on a flat knit row and knit the tails in with the new stitches.  It can have a little more bulk if the yarn is too heavy or bulky.
3. **RUSSIAN JOIN or a SPLICING TYPE JOIN** - Another way to join is the Russian join, which uses a tapestry needle. And weaving the spliced ends together.  It is hard to do this for a precise color change and should really only use this method for animal fibers, as it may not hold up in multiple washings.  Be sure to use plenty of tail here for a good hold. A "spit-splice" is similar to Russian but can ONLY be used on animal fiber.

Here is my video on using a knot to join the yarn.
Loom Knit: How to Change Colors[114].

## S LOOM and AFGHAN LOOMS

S-looms can be quite big and hard to get used to since they can produce a panel around 60" wide (more or less for some models). The looms can fit across the lap or on a table. Many times it can be easier to turn the loom vertical and rotate the shape to get a better angle for wrapping or knitting.  This can be frustrating for some or downright impossible for others with dexterity issues.  If you are looking to purchase an Afghan loom I would suggest first reading reviews and checking message boards, watch video reviews and tips from various people, asking a friend if they have one and their opinion if possible, and lastly testing out the loom in a store if possible (see if you can bring in your own yarn to practice just wrapping the loom) or borrowing from a friend. These looms are wonderful at what they provide but be sure you really like to work on large projects before impulse buying.

An S loom, Infinity, Afghan or large panel loom are set up for single or flat panel knitting. However some are set up already for double knitting or you CAN make double knit items with the right setup and super bulky yarn (or a few strands of bulky). Here is one for the Knitting Board S loom.

Double Knit setup: KnittingBoard Super Afghan S loom[115].

## LOOSE END/EDGE?

Is that beginning side of your knitting loose and ugly?  Check this tip out and fix it!

Loom Knit Finish off Beginning Loose End of Panel[116].

## KITCHENER STITCH (close sock, etc)

Stitch together socks and more with the Kitchener stitch.

Loom Knit: Kitchener Stitch or invisible stitch (socks, panel, headband)[117].

## 3 STRANDS FROM 1 BALL of YARN!

Yarn tip to get more out of the low priced worsted with yarn

Yarn – Make 3 strands from 1 ball Navajo technique (CC)[118].

## STITCHES TO CAST ON?

How do I get things the right size or find out how many stitches to cast on? See **Knitter's Math and Charts** Chapter for formulas and clear explanations. Includes help on how much yarn you used or need for a project, too!

Make a Swatch – Check Knitting Gauge or measure gauge (CC)[119].

## POM POMS

Make a pom pom by hand without a tool besides your yarn and scissors…and your hands!

Crafts: How to Make an easy PomPom[120].

## Curl Up and Dye! Knitting that Curls

Prevent knits from curling and your friends and loved ones will appreciate the extra care you took. If not, they don't deserve it anyways! No, seriously. I know people get mortified to see their knit roll up and can say it happened to me, too. Let's chat about why it happens, how to prevent curling to start and also how to fix the mistake AFTER it happens. Most importantly read how to prevent it from happening in the first place.

A quick note before continuing: Many stitch patterns that do not curl. As the beginner gets more comfortable he/she will notice that there are more stitches than just e-wrap in loom knitting. This section is all about learning the basics in troubleshooting curling, which is common when just learning to knit.

**The WHY:**
You just knit your first __(FILL IN THE BLANK)__ and it won't stop curling! If you didn't know before, now you know that all knit stitches on one side of the fabric will curl. It's called stockinette, but that is not very comforting when you are staring at this beautiful blanket you just spent weeks or months making for your loved one. What is stockinette? It is the name of the word for the stitch pattern of all knit stitches. The stitches all curl in the same direction when made. The V that is created in the front of the fabric actually bends toward the back and looks like a bar or "bump" in the back. That stitch in the back is a purl stitch. It is the exact opposite of a knit stitch in which way it bends.

*All knit stitches are called "stockinette". Stockinette knitting will curl."*

Another way to say it; when the "RS" or Right Side of your knitting is all knit stitches, whether they are standard or twisted (E-wrap on loom or ktbl for needles) knit stitches, the fabric will curl. Since all of the stitches bend toward the back of your knitting this happens. When all purls are used on the RS then we call this "reverse stockinette".

**The HOW (to prevent):**
To prevent knits from curling, add purl stitches. These fight or skew in the opposite direction. A "reverse stockinette" is made from all purl stitches on the right side (front) of the work. Changing the stitch pattern on the ends and edges will prevent curling.

Stitch patterns to prevent curling, that are commonly used, would be:
• garter stitch
• ribbing (1×1, 2×2 3×3 or other combos alternating sets of knits & purls)
• seed stitches
• moss stitches

Here are some common crochet edges followed by common ends and edges to work into your projects. The crochet edges are added after your stockinette is all made. The knit edges are something you'll want to plan on from the beginning of your project.

**Crochet:**
Double Crochet[121]
Texture Stitch[122]
*Add these after your stockinette is knitted and complete.*

**Knit Stitch patterns:**
Garter[123]
Rib[124]
Seed[125]
Moss[126]
*Cast on and work an edge about 1" (or desired amount) of one the above patterns. On the next row use the first 5 stitches* (or enough for 1") in the same pattern as the end. On the last 5 stitches* repeat the same pattern. Continue in your stockinette until 1" before binding off. Add 1" more in the same stitch pattern and bind off. Your knitting should not curl. If the border was not quite wide enough then blocking should fix the rest. See **Blocking** below.*

**What if my work is finished and I want to fix it AFTER it's all done?**
Stop project from curling after it's knit:
1. **Crochet edge** - If you can learn or know some simple crochet, you can add a crochet edge. This will prevent knits from curling after the fact. Try a double crochet edge, a texture stitch pattern, or other decorative stitch patterns.
2. **Add border to selvedge edge and ends after made** - You can hang the edge or end stitches back on your loom and start knitting one of the above stitch patterns; There is no need to cast on, simply hang the edge stitches on each peg and begin knitting and purling. This creates a non-rolling or non-curling border. Bind off again and weave in all tails.

3. **Make a hem**! If you have enough extra fabric made (say your hat is a 1″ or so longer than needed or your blanket or panel is a few inches too wide or long) then you can also fold over your knitting and sew it with matching yarn and a wide-eyed tapestry needle. [Think of a hemmed brim of an easy beanie hat.  The stitches aren't being placed back on the pegs but sewn in on the backside AFTER your knitting is complete.]

    a. **Turn fabric to wrong side and fold back to make a hem**. Sew consistently the same spacing into the back of the stitches.  I recommend sewing through the purl bump along the back.  Sew it the same and with consistency along that edge so your knitting will look even.  TIP!! If you have a hard time measuring how much to fold over, try cutting a jig or template.

    b. **To make a template:** Use a long piece of smooth wood, heavy poster board, cardboard, etc or even a thin piece of plastic as a guide. Cut to the desired hem width.  Lay this template inside the part that is folded and leave a thumbs-worth sticking out the end that you are sewing toward.  Pull the template out as you go and continue sewing.  At corners you'll need to fold and tack down one corner lightly first before folding over the other side or it will be bulky looking.

Again, this is a fix for after your knitting is complete and if you have enough room to be short on your project length.

**Blocking:**
Wet blocking or steam blocking can help some slight curling from happening.  However be careful when using steam.  Too much heat on an acrylic can "kill" the yarn and wool with heat and friction can cause felting.  Wet blocking is the best way to block any fiber with out risk to ruin your knitting. For more why's on blocking and "How To" see **Wet Block Your Knitting**.

# Wet Block Your Knitting

"Block your knitting" may sound scary or foreign but the fact is it can make your project sing! It will help the stitches even out and any open lace-work and define features like cables nicely.

*"Even the professionals block"*

There are ways to steam knitting that can kill synthetic yarns but **Wet Blocking** I've found is perfect for all types of yarn. It is also inexpensive and simple. Some methods of blocking could have too high of heat or too much friction for the fiber in your project. With the following method avoids damage to any project.

*"A simple wet block to knitting evens your work."*

### Wet Blocking Instructions:

This method is safe for all types of yarn.
Before starting you'll want to read the care instruction on your yarn. If it is a natural fiber or the instructions say to hand wash do not use a machine to wet your project. If you have a machine washable fiber you can run it through the wash on gentle then follow pinning instructions below; if the item has lacework simply wash by hand with a recommended mild detergent then follow pinning instructions below as with the natural fiber or hand-wash yarn.

### Washing Instructions:

*Before starting with hand dyed fibers you may need to test your yarn for color fastness or use only water and vinegar to set the color.*

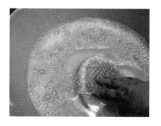

Need: Gentle detergent use to wash delicates, a clean sink or basin, clean water and dry white towels. I prefer to wash by hand in a plastic basin with a mild product called Soak. This detergent is formulated to not need rinsing. (Other great brands are available, too).

- Mix with one tsp of detergent (or vinegar) to 1 gallon of water. Use spring or filtered tap; this keeps you knitting from any harsh or hard elements that could be in the tap water. Clean water is especially important for very light yarns.
- Mix together with your hand in a clean sink or basin. Place knitting in and let soak in for 15 minutes or until the water is fully absorbed into the yarn.
- Gently squeeze out the water.
- Place in a dry white towel, roll and gently press down. Knitting will be damp. Unroll and repeat. Knitting should be damp, not soaking or dry.

**Pinning instructions:**
Need:

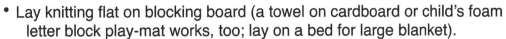

1. Blocking Board(s) or clean kids play-mats; these are plastic mats that interlock together. If item is too large use a bed.
2. Rust resistant T-pins or other blocking pin sets; these are reusable.
3. Blocking wires (if long item it saves on t-pins); purchase online or local yarn stores.
4. Optional: may want a spray bottle with more clean water to dampen any fast drying spots again.

- Lay knitting flat on blocking board (a towel on cardboard or child's foam letter block play-mat works, too; lay on a bed for large blanket).
- Pin the corners evenly with 1 pin in each corner.
- On one side start pinning behind each edge to have a nice straight line. If there are embellishments like a picot or lacy edge work, pin those points or openings to reveal the stitch work.
- Adjust corner pins as necessary.
- Repeat for adjacent side and work your way to the corner opposite your first starting pin. Try to match the sizing pinned from the first side.
- Now skip the next side and go to the side opposite the end you just pinned.
- After pinning behind each feature or edging (picot edge example photo), adjust the pins as needed and complete the last side.

For small items that need shape use clean water spray bottle to spray onto your knitting. For form fitted items place over a bowl, drinking glass, dish or even a balloon. This can give some shape to your knitting as it dries.

Leave knitting until it is dry. Be sure to place in a well-ventilated area with good air circulation.

127

How to Wet Block

# Travel With Knitting

Want to travel and take along your projects? The following list is compiled from polling many contributors in the GKK Facebook Club, experience and research. This is an abbreviated list but the entire article, with personal stories, can be found on the goodknitkisses.com website.

## General tips for traveling on airplanes:

1. First read the tsa.gov website or catsa.gc.ca for current regulations (or your country of arrival/departure). This is important due to change over time. PRINT the guidelines and carry with you if the question arrises at the checkpoint; have it ready. Do not argue with the officer but the paper could come in handy if there is question. If you travel frequently consider laminating the paper and placing in you project bag.
2. If you're still in doubt, call the airline(s) in advance to check their rules.
3. If you unsure of bringing an item, either leave it at home or check your baggage under the aircraft. Choose a less expensive travel version if it is likely to get confiscated on the initial or return flight.
4. Scissors: Less than 4 in. (10 cm) metal scissors are allowed in the U.S. for travel and 6 in.(15.24 cm) for Canada. Yarn cutters, also called circular thread cutters, many times are not allowed due to an open razor blade inside. *An alternate cutting tool, that is acceptable, are sharp nail clippers.*
5. Loom hooks or pick: Most have no trouble carrying these with their knitting. However some travelers have had their nice picks confiscated from time to time. Take a few less expensive picks for travel or consider a bent needle. There are metal ones that are sturdy and plastic are also available. An unfolded large paperclip works as well if all else fails.
6. Looms: Use caution when packing plastic looms that are checked or carry-on. But most looms do not have a problem whether metal, wood or plastic. Have a bit of knitting hanging on the loom. Then if they ask you what it is you have the pattern and example there on the loom.

## Helpful websites for the U.S.:

http://www.tsa.gov/traveler-information/prohibited-items[128]

www.tsa.gov/traveler-information/transporting-knitting-needles-and-needlepoint[129]

# Chapter 4
## Gauge

The Gauge of Knitting is the measurement of stitches after your main stitch pattern has been knitted with a specific yarn. The sample is usually blocked and dry before measuring (see **Blocking**).

The gauge size is determined by the tool used (see **Loom Gauge**), yarn weight, stitch method, knitter's tension, and knitter's mood. To make sure your knitting will be the same size as the pattern, you will want to knit a sample on the loom, with the yarn, and main stitch intended for the project (see **Why Swatch**).

Thankfully there are more and more knitting looms on the market everyday. Even if your loom, or the loom called for in a pattern, becomes discontinued you can still figure out which loom to use. You can also see if more or less stitches are needed to get the right size by making a swatch (see **Knitter's Math section** and **Why Swatch**) or making an educated decision with the following info.

**Needle Patterns** - If you are converting a needle-knitting pattern to the loom, use our short chart as a guide! Notice the columns with the Needle Equivalent listed and stitches per inch. Also included are recommended yarn weights for the needles and looms "C2C" or "Gauge" listed. These appear in a range of needles & weights as your loom can handle different stitches per inch with a change in yarn, stitch pattern, and tension (how tight or loose you tend to knit). Please note that the US and UK/AU systems are noted. For stitches per inch in metric, multiply the number by 4. That will give you 4", which is 10 cm. Your new number will be roughly the number of stitches in a 10 cm swatch. (2.54cm = 1 inch). Keep in mind that stitches per inch listed are taken from averages and are not set in stone. The rows per inch are not listed on this chart. Use the C2C or Gauge on larger master charts on the following pages.

| Needle Range | C2C | Gauge | Yarn Weight Range (UK/AU) | Average sts per in | Crochet (US) |
|---|---|---|---|---|---|
| 1 - 3 (2.25 mm/3.25 mm) | 3/16" | EFG | US 0 - 2 ( 1-3 ply) | 7 - 8 sts | A - D |
| 3 - 6 (3.25 mm/4 mm) | 1/4" | FG | US 1 - 3 ( 2-4 ply & 8 ply) | 5 - 7 sts | D - G |
| 5 - 8 (3.75 mm/5 mm) | 5/16", 3/8", 7/16" | SG | US 2 - 4 ( 2-4 ply, 8 ply & DK) | 4 - 5 sts | F - H |
| 8 - 10 (5 mm/6 mm) | 1/2", 9/16" | RG | US 4 - 5 ( 8 - 12 ply, DK, Aran) | 3 - 4 sts | H - J |
| 10 - 13 (6 mm/9 mm) | 5/8", 11/16" | LG | US 5 - 6 ( 10 - 12 ply, Aran, Chk) | 2 - 3 sts | J - M |
| 13 - 15 (9 mm/10 mm) | 3/4", 13/16", 7/8", 15/16" | XLG | US 6 - 7 ( 12 ply & Chunky) | 1.5 - 3 sts | M - N+ |
| 19 - 35 (12.75 mm/20+) | +/- 1 1/2" | JUMBO | US 6 - 7 ( Chunky & Roving) | .75 - 1 sts | M - Q+ |

**Loom Gauge** - Loom gauge is the distance the yarn travels from one peg to another which makes up 1 stitch. The measurement from the center of one peg to the next is called C2C Peg Spacing (Center to Center). Some looms with peg and pin systems do not measure C2C. Also, the diameter of a peg can change the gauge. The distance from center to center determines the classification of a loom into a category.

The loom gauge categories actually are determined by manufacturer(s) test knitting several swatches (samples) in appropriate yarn to see which category that loom should fall under. The categories actually line up with a range of needle sizes. Keep this page handy as well when converting needle patterns.

| Loom Gauge Categories: | Approximate Needle Equivalent: |
|---|---|
| EFG = Extra Fine Gauge (3/16″) | 1-3 (2.25mm – 3.25mm) |
| FG = Fine Gauge (1/4″) | 3-6 (3.25mm – 4mm) |
| SG = Small Gauge (5/16″, 3/8″, 7/16″) | 6-8 (3.75mm – 5mm) |
| RG = Regular Gauge (1/2″, 9/16″) | 8-10 (5mm – 6mm) |
| LG = Large Gauge (5/8″, 11/16″) | 10-13 (6mm – 9mm) |
| XLG = Extra Large (3/4″, 3/16″,7/8″,15/16″) | 13-15 (9mm – 10mm) |
| JUMBO* = EXL+ to Jumbo (+/- 1 1/2″) | 19-35+ (12.75mm – 20+mm) |

*Not official name; works with Jumbo #7 U.S. yarn weight.

## Manufacturer Notes on Loom Gauge

Most manufacturers determine their gauge/set of their knitting loom product and will list it with the Loom Gauge abbreviation and/or the C2C fraction. If it is not listed you can usually measure this for yourself or check our chart. There are a few exceptions though. Different looms will have pegs of various diameters or even peg and pin systems (Kiss-looms) that make it hard to measure and also can change the gauge from one peg to the next.

## Patterns Notes for Loom Gauge

If a manufacturer writes the loom gauge, they may not always write" C2C"; it may be only written with a fraction number or the category name. This term, C2C, is used to explain HOW to measure. In loom patterns it may be written as a fraction, abbreviation or a specific loom may be called out. Look in the C2C chart column for the general category name.

## Loom Comparison Examples

- Loom A & B are listed as SG and 3/8". They can both be measured from the center of the peg groove to the center of the next peg groove. However, Loom B's peg is just a little bit larger in diameter than Loom A. Here the stitches per inch *could* be slightly less on Loom B compared to a swatch from Loom A with the same yarn and type of stitch pattern.
- Loom C is a Kiss loom with a peg in front and a pin behind on a thinner pin board; this loom is listed as an SG but it is difficult to measure. Here the yarn travels in front of the peg and then behind the pin that is behind and offset from the peg. The distance between the peg and pin can get larger if washers are added between the front larger board and the thin pin board to change the overall gauge. *Knitting a swatch (see **Why Swatch**) is the best way to confirm overall knit gauge.*

Again, other contributing parts to determine the gauge of knitting are: Yarn weight, stitch, tension and your mood. Your knitting gauge can be different than a fellow knitter due to these even on the same loom!

Adjustable Looms

This is an exciting feature but should come with an explanation as to what the word "adjustable" means. Adjustable can be a deceiving word. Most looms have a fixed number of pegs and a rigid frame. However, there are a few looms that can adjust the actual size of he stitches on the same loom.

Here are examples of how the word adjustable should be used:
1   If a **frame** can be adjusted to change the number of pegs then we would say it is *Adjustable Size Only*.
2   If you can choose between two or more gauges and it is also peg count adjustable we would say it is *Size Adjustable & 2+ gauges*.
3   If the distance between the pegs can be changed slowly with washers then we would say the loom is *Size and Gauge Adjustable*. Size adjustable looms allow the knitter to slide or move part of the frame to get the desired peg count.

# LOOM GAUGE CHART

The following Chart contains popular looms on the market. A few may be discontinued but are in many homes due to popularity; thousands of patterns have been written for these looms and therefore are on the chart for reference. Brand/Manufacturer sorts this chart.

The following chart is so large that it is broken into 4 charts to fit. For a free downloadable PDF of charts in this book check the first link found in "Endnotes". Endnotes are on the last pages of this book. The first link will take you to a website. There you can download the charts and use clickable endnotes corresponding to endnote numbers in the book.

*Measurements included are taken from a hard ruler or a digital caliper for accuracy on actual looms; you can do this on your own looms for looms not listed.

**Brands included:**
- Kiss Looms (Size and Gauge adjustable; custom available)
- Knifty Knitter (ProvoCraft – no longer in production; loom clips can adjust long loom peg count in the round; nick name KK).
- Knitting Board (also called KB or AKB Authentic Knitting Board; double knit, single, circular, weave and some adjustable **size** type looms).
- Knitting Frame Noble Knitter (nickname Noble Knitter)
- Loops & Threads (Michael's Looms; similar to Hobby Lobby Looms; see Boye or Knifty Knitter similar patterns).
- Lion Brand Martha Stewart Loom Knit & Weave Kit (adjustable size & 2 gauges+ to knit or weave; nickname MS).

This is not an extensive or inclusive list worldwide. Many looms are made by hand or are ones that we don't have the looms to verify. However the notes here should help you determine your loom gauge or help find a better fit for your pattern. Additional notes: The Yarnology rectangular long loom set is identical to the 4 Knifty Knitter gauges and peg count in chart. Knit UK looms and Cottage looms are also not included in the chart.

## Loom Gauge Chart

| Brand | Loom Name/Type | Color/Mat. | Peg/Pin | Pairs | Pegs | Gauge | C2C |
|---|---|---|---|---|---|---|---|
| Boye | Scarf Loom | red | plastic | 18 | 18 | XLG | 13/16" |
| Boye | Long Loom | blue | plastic | 12 | 26 | LG | 11/16" |
| Boye | Long Loom | green | plastic | 18 | 38 | LG | 11/16" |
| Boye | Long Loom | pink | plastic | 24 | 50 | LG | 11/16" |
| Boye | Long Loom | orange | plastic | 30 | 62 | LG | 11/16" |
| Boye | Flower Loom | bright blue | plastic | - | 12 | XLG | 3/4" |
| Boye | Small Round Loom | bright green | plastic | - | 24 | LG | 5/8" |
| Boye | Medium Round Loom | bright blue | plastic | - | 30 | LG | 11/16" |
| Boye | Large Round Loom | brt orange | plastic | - | 36 | XLG | 3/4" |
| Boye | Extra Large Round Loom | bright pink | plastic | - | 40 | XLG | 7/8" |
| CinDWood Crafts | Thumb Loom (2 1/5") | MDF | nylon | - | 8 | LG | 5/8" |
| CinDWood Crafts | Thumb Loom (2 1/5") | MDF | nylon | - | 10 | RG | 1/2" |
| CinDWood Crafts | Preemie Bootie Loom (2 1/2") | MDF | nylon | - | 10 | LG | 5/8" |
| CinDWood Crafts | Preemie Bootie Loom (2 1/2") | MDF | nylon | - | 12 | RG | 1/2" |
| CinDWood Crafts | Newborn Bootie Loom (3") | MDF | nylon | - | 10 | XLG | 3/4" |
| CinDWood Crafts | Newborn Bootie Loom (3") | MDF | nylon | - | 12 | LG | 5/8" |
| CinDWood Crafts | Newborn Bootie Loom (3") | MDF | nylon | - | 14 | RG | 1/2" |
| CinDWood Crafts | Small Baby Bootie Loom (31/2") | MDF | nylon | - | 12 | XLG | 3/4" |
| CinDWood Crafts | Small Baby Bootie Loom (31/2") | MDF | nylon | - | 18 | RG | 1/2" |
| CinDWood Crafts | Baby Bootie Loom (4") | MDF | nylon | - | 14 | XLG | 3/4" |
| CinDWood Crafts | Baby Bootie Loom (4") | MDF | nylon | - | 16 | LG | 5/8" |
| CinDWood Crafts | Baby Bootie Loom (4") | MDF | nylon | - | 20 | RG | 1/2" |
| CinDWood Crafts | Child Bootie Loom (4 4/5") | MDF | nylon | - | 18 | XLG | 3/4" |
| CinDWood Crafts | Child Bootie Loom (4 4/5") | MDF | nylon | - | 20 | LG | 5/8" |
| CinDWood Crafts | Child Bootie Loom (4 4/5") | MDF | nylon | - | 24 | RG | 1/2" |
| CinDWood Crafts | Youth Bootie Loom (4 4/5") | MDF | nylon | - | 27 | RG | 1/2" |
| CinDWood Crafts | Adult Bootie Loom (5 3/8") | MDF | nylon | - | 20 | XLG | 3/4" |
| CinDWood Crafts | Adult Bootie Loom (5 3/8") | MDF | nylon | - | 24 | LG | 5/8" |
| CinDWood Crafts | Adult Bootie Loom (5 3/8") | MDF | nylon | - | 30 | RG | 1/2" |
| CinDWood Crafts | Adult Sock Loom (1 size) | MDF | nylon | - | 40 | SG | 3/8" |
| CinDWood Crafts | Knitted Knocker Loom (Fine Gauge) | MDF | nylon | - | 56 | FG | 1/4" |
| CinDWood Crafts | Adult Hat Loom (Small Gauge) | MDF | nylon | - | 80 | SG | 3/8" |
| CinDWood Crafts | Adult Hat Loom (Fine Gauge) | MDF | nylon | - | 120 | FG | 1/4" |
| CinDWood Crafts | Preemie Hat Loom 2-5 pounds (5 3/8") | MDF | nylon | - | 20 | XLG | 3/4" |
| CinDWood Crafts | Preemie Hat Loom 2-5 pounds (5 3/8") | MDF | nylon | - | 24 | LG | 5/8" |
| CinDWood Crafts | Preemie Hat Loom 2-5 pounds (5 3/8") | MDF | nylon | - | 30 | RG | 1/2" |
| CinDWood Crafts | Preemie Hat Loom 3-6 pounds (6") | MDF | nylon | - | 22 | XLG | 3/4" |
| CinDWood Crafts | Preemie Hat Loom 3-6 pounds (6") | MDF | nylon | - | 33 | RG | 1/2" |
| CinDWood Crafts | Newborn Hat Loom 5-8 pounds (6 1/2") | MDF | nylon | - | 24 | XLG | 3/4" |
| CinDWood Crafts | Newborn Hat Loom 5-8 pounds (6 1/2") | MDF | nylon | - | 30 | LG | 5/8" |
| CinDWood Crafts | Newborn Hat Loom 5-8 pounds (6 1/2") | MDF | nylon | - | 36 | RG | 1/2" |
| CinDWood Crafts | Baby Hat Loom 3-18 mths (7 1/2") | MDF | nylon | - | 27 | XLG | 3/4" |

GUIDE: Use Chart to convert needle patterns to best loom & yarn.  Look at stitches per inch and needle size.  Test the yarn on your loom with a gauge swatch.  Adjust yarn to thinner for more sts per in or thicker for less. Wash or block swatch before measuring for accuaracy.

| Needle Range | C2C | Gauge | | Yarn Weight Range (UK/AU) | Average sts per in | Crochet (US) |
|---|---|---|---|---|---|---|
| 1 - 3 (2.25 mm/3.25 mm) | 3/10" | EFG | | US 0 - 0 ( 1-3 ply) | 7 - 8 sts | A - D |
| 3 - 6 (3.25 mm/4 mm) | 1/4" | FG | | US 1 - 3 ( 2-4 ply & 8 ply) | 5 - 7 sts | D - G |
| 5 - 8 (3.75 mm/5 mm) | 5/16", 3/8", 7/16" | SG | | US 2 - 4 ( 2-4 ply, 8 ply & DK) | 4 - 5 sts | F - H |
| 8 - 10 (5 mm/6 mm) | 1/2", 9/16" | RG | | US 4 - 5 ( 8 - 12 ply, DK, Aran) | 3 - 4 sts | H - J |
| 10 - 13 (6 mm/9 mm) | 5/8", 11/16" | LG | | US 5 - 6 ( 10 - 12 ply, Aran, Chk) | 2 - 3 sts | J - M |
| 13 - 15 (9 mm/10 mm) | 3/4", 13/16", 7/8", 15/16" | XLG | | US 6 - 7 ( 12 ply & Chunky) | 1.5 - 3 sts | M - N+ |
| 19 - 35 (12.75 mm/20+) | +/- 1 1/2" | JUMBO | | US 6 - 7 ( Chunky & Roving) | .75 - 1 sts | M - Q+ |

**EFG=Extra Fine Gauge I FG=Fine Gauge I SG=Small Gauge I RG=Regular Gauge I LG=Large Gauge I XLG=Extra Large Gauge I JUMBO=Extra Large Gauge+**

**Chart Copyright 2015 GoodKnit Kisses; for personal use. *Not an exhaustive list; contact if errors; not all Brands are still in production.**

## Loom Gauge Chart

| Brand | Loom Name/Type | Color/Mat. | Peg | Pairs | Pegs | Gauge | C2C |
|---|---|---|---|---|---|---|---|
| CinDWood Crafts | Baby Hat Loom 3-18 mths (7 1/2") | MDF | nylon | - | 32 | LG | 5/8" |
| CinDWood Crafts | Baby Hat Loom 3-18 mths (7 1/2") | MDF | nylon | - | 40 | RG | 1/2" |
| CinDWood Crafts | Child Hat Loom 2-6 years (8") | MDF | nylon | - | 30 | XLG | 3/4" |
| CinDWood Crafts | Child Hat Loom 2-6 years (8") | MDF | nylon | - | 36 | LG | 5/8" |
| CinDWood Crafts | Child Hat Loom 2-6 years (8") | MDF | nylon | - | 44 | RG | 1/2" |
| CinDWood Crafts | Youth Hat Loom 7-12 years (9") | MDF | nylon | - | 34 | XLG | 3/4" |
| CinDWood Crafts | Youth Hat Loom 7-12 years (9") | MDF | nylon | - | 42 | LG | 5/8" |
| CinDWood Crafts | Youth Hat Loom 7-12 years (9") | MDF | nylon | - | 50 | RG | 1/2" |
| CinDWood Crafts | Youth Hat Loom 12-17 years (9 3/4") | MDF | nylon | - | 36 | XLG | 3/4" |
| CinDWood Crafts | Youth Hat Loom 12-17 years (9 3/4") | MDF | nylon | - | 44 | LG | 5/8" |
| CinDWood Crafts | Youth Hat Loom 12-17 years (9 3/4") | MDF | nylon | - | 56 | RG | 1/2" |
| CinDWood Crafts | Adult Hat loom (10 1/2") | MDF | nylon | - | 40 | XLG | 3/4" |
| CinDWood Crafts | *Adult Hat loom (10 1/2")=48 peg purple | MDF | nylon | - | 48 | LG | 5/8" |
| CinDWood Crafts | Adult Hat loom (10 1/2") | MDF | nylon | - | 60 | RG | 1/2" |
| CinDWood Crafts | Large Adult Hat Loom (11 1/2") | MDF | nylon | - | 42 | XLG | 3/4" |
| CinDWood Crafts | Large Adult Hat Loom (11 1/2") | MDF | nylon | - | 54 | LG | 5/8" |
| CinDWood Crafts | Large Adult Hat Loom (11 1/2") | MDF | nylon | - | 66 | RG | 1/2" |
| CinDWood Crafts | Oval Adult Hat Loom | MDF | nylon | - | 41 | XLG | 3/4" |
| CinDWood Crafts | Oval Adult Hat Loom | MDF | nylon | - | 60 | RG | 1/2" |
| CinDWood Crafts | Oval Youth Hat Loom 7-12 years | MDF | nylon | - | 35 | XLG | 3/4" |
| CinDWood Crafts | Oval Youth Hat Loom 7-12 years | MDF | nylon | - | 51 | RG | 1/2" |
| CinDWood Crafts | Oval Youth Lg Hat Loom 12-17 years | MDF | nylon | - | 37 | XLG | 3/4" |
| CinDWood Crafts | Oval Youth Lg Hat Loom 12-17 years | MDF | nylon | - | 55 | RG | 1/2" |
| CinDWood Crafts | 4" Mini Narrow Scarf Loom (fig 8 wrap) | MDF | nylon | - | 12 | RG | 1/2" |
| CinDWood Crafts | 6" Scarf Loom Narrow (fig 8 wrap) | MDF | nylon | - | 24 | RG | 1/2" |
| CinDWood Crafts | 12" Scarf Loom Narrow (fig 8 wrap) | MDF | nylon | - | 46 | RG | 1/2" |
| CinDWood Crafts | 24" Oval/Panel Loom + wedge | MDF | nylon | - | 82 | LG | 5/8" |
| CinDWood Crafts | 24" Oval/Panel Loom + wedge | MDF | nylon | - | 104 | RG | 1/2" |
| CinDWood Crafts | 36" Oval/Panel Loom + wedge | MDF | nylon | - | 120 | LG | 5/8" |
| CinDWood Crafts | 36" Oval/Panel Loom + wedge | MDF | nylon | - | 146 | RG | 1/2" |
| CinDWood Crafts | 20" Round Afghan Loom | MDF | nylon | - | 80 | XLG | 3/4" |
| CinDWood Crafts | 20" Round Afghan Loom | MDF | nylon | - | 100 | LG | 5/8" |
| CinDWood Crafts | 20" Round Afghan Loom | MDF | nylon | - | 120 | RG | 1/2" |
| CinDWood Crafts | Oval Afghan Loom | MDF | nylon | - | 78 | XLG | 3/4" |
| CinDWood Crafts | Oval Afghan Loom | MDF | nylon | - | 116 | RG | 1/2" |
| CinDWood Crafts | 15" Small Round Afghan Loom | MDF | nylon | - | 60 | XLG | 3/4" |
| CinDWood Crafts | 15" Small Round Afghan Loom | MDF | nylon | - | 74 | LG | 5/8" |
| CinDWood Crafts | 15" Small Round Afghan Loom | MDF | nylon | - | 90 | RG | 1/2" |
| CinDWood Crafts | Afghan Square Loom | MDF | nylon | - | 15 | LG | 5/8" |
| CinDWood Crafts | Afghan Square Loom | MDF | nylon | - | 19 | RG | 1/2" |
| CinDWood Crafts - "S" shape | 36" Universal S-Curve Panel Loom +w. | MDF | nylon | 49 | 118 | LG | 5/8" |
| CinDWood Crafts - "S" shape | 48" Universal S-Curve Panel Loom+w. | MDF | nylon | 63 | 147 | LG | 5/8" |

GUIDE: Use Chart to convert needle patterns to best loom & yarn.  Look at stitches per inch and needle size.  Test the yarn on your loom with a gauge swatch.  Adjust yarn to thinner for more sts per in or thicker for less. Wash or block swatch before measuring for accuracy.

| Needle Range | C2C | Gauge |
|---|---|---|
| 1 - 3 (2.25 mm/3.25 mm) | 3/16" | EFG |
| 3 - 6 (3.25 mm/4 mm) | 1/4" | FG |
| 5 - 8 (3.75 mm/5 mm) | 5/16", 3/8", 7/16" | SG |
| 8 - 10 (5 mm/6 mm) | 1/2", 9/16" | RG |
| 10 - 13 (6 mm/9 mm) | 5/8", 11/16" | LG |
| 13 - 15 (9 mm/10 mm) | 3/4", 13/16", 7/8", 15/16" | XLG |
| 19 - 35 (12.75 mm/20+) | +/- 1 1/2" | JUMBO |

| Yarn Weight Range (UK/AU) | Average sts per in | Crochet (US) |
|---|---|---|
| US 0 - 2 ( 1-3 ply) | 7 - 8 sts | A - D |
| US 1 - 3 ( 2-4 ply & 8 ply) | 5 - 7 sts | D - G |
| US 2 - 4 ( 2-4 ply, 8 ply & DK) | 4 - 5 sts | F - H |
| US 4 - 5 ( 8 - 12 ply, DK, Aran) | 3 - 4 sts | H - J |
| US 5 - 6 ( 10 - 12 ply, Aran, Chk) | 2 - 3 sts | J - M |
| US 6 - 7 ( 12 ply & Chunky) | 1.5 - 3 sts | M - N+ |
| US 6 - 7 ( Chunky & Roving) | .75 - 1 sts | M - Q+ |

**EFG=Extra Fine Gauge I FG=Fine Gauge I SG=Small Gauge I RG=Regular Gauge I LG=Large Gauge I XLG=Extra Large Gauge I JUMBO=Extra Large Gauge+**
**Chart Copyright 2015 GoodKnit Kisses; for personal use. *Not an exhaustive list; contact if errors; not all Brands are still in production.**

## Loom Gauge Chart

| Brand | Loom Name/Type | Color | Peg | Pairs | Pegs | Gauge | C2C |
|---|---|---|---|---|---|---|---|
| CinDWood Crafts - "S" shape | 60" Universal S-Curve Panel Loom+w. | MDF | nylon | 84 | 197 | LG | 5/8" |
| CinDWood Crafts - "S" shape | 36" Universal S-Curve Panel Loom +w. | MDF | nylon | 59 | 150 | RG | 1/2" |
| CinDWood Crafts - "S" shape | 48" Universal S-Curve Panel Loom+w. | MDF | nylon | 84 | 192 | RG | 1/2" |
| CinDWood Crafts - "S" shape | 60" Universal S-Curve Panel Loom+w. | MDF | nylon | 104 | 248 | RG | 1/2" |
| CinDWood Crafts (Size Adj) | Universal 15" Hat/Scarf Loom +wedge | MDF | nylon | 22 | 52 | LG | 5/8" |
| CinDWood Crafts (Size Adj) | Universal 15" Hat/Scarf Loom+ wedge | MDF | nylon | 28 | 64 | RG | 1/2" |
| Horizon Laptop Knit & Loom | Rectangle | pink | plastic | - | 32 | RG | 1/2" |
| Horizon Laptop Knit & Loom | Round Loom (inner circle) | purple | plastic | - | 24 | XLG | 3/4" |
| Horizon Laptop Knit & Loom | Round Loom (inner circle) | purple | plastic | - | 28 | XLG | 3/4" |
| Horizon Laptop Knit & Loom | Round Loom (inner circle) | purple | plastic | - | 32 | XLG | 3/4" |
| Horizon Laptop Knit & Loom | Round Loom (outer circle) | green | plastic | - | 36 | XLG | 3/4" |
| Horizon Laptop Knit & Loom | Round Loom (outer circle) | green | plastic | - | 48 | LG | 5/8" |
| Horizon Laptop Knit & Loom | Round Loom (outer circle) | green | plastic | - | 44 | XLG | 3/4" |
| Kiss Looms (Size Adj only) | Fixed 0 Sock Loom | Maple | Brass | - | 12 min - custom | EFG | 3/16" |
| Kiss Looms (Size Adj only) | Fixed 1 Sock Loom | Maple | Brass | - | 12 min - custom | EFG-FG | 1/4" |
| Kiss Looms (Size Adj only) | Fixed 2 Sock Loom | Maple | Brass | - | 12 min - custom | FG-SG | 1/4" |
| Kiss Looms (Size & Gauge adj) | Small Gauge Adjustable + 0 washers | Maple | Brass | 14-77 | 30 – 216 | SG Adj + 0 | 3/8"" * |
| Kiss Looms (Size & Gauge adj) | Small Gauge Adjustable +2 washers | Maple | Brass | 14-77 | 30 – 216 | SG Adj + 2 =RG | 1/2" * |
| Kiss Looms (Size & Gauge adj) | Small Gauge Adjustable +6-7 washers | Maple | Brass | 14-77 | 30 – 216 | SG Adj + 6 to 7 = XLG | 3/4" * |
| Kiss Looms (Size & Gauge adj) | Regular Gauge Adjustable+ 0 washers | Maple | Brass | 9-53 | 20 – 148 | RG Adj + 0 | 1/2" * |
| Kiss Looms (Size & Gauge adj) | Regular Gauge Adjustable +5-6 wash. | Maple | Brass | 9-53 | 20 – 148 | RG Adj +5 to 6 = XLG | 3/4" * |
| Kiss Looms (Size & Gauge adj) | Modular +0 washers | Maple | Brass | 6-60 | 6 – 240** | RG Adj | 1/2" * |
| Kiss Looms (Size & Gauge adj) | Modular +5 or 6 washers | Maple | Brass | 6-60 | 6 – 240** | RG Adj +5 to 6 = XLG | 3/4" * |
| Kiss Looms (Size Adj only) | Dragon Loom | Maple | Brass | - | 24-42 | LG - XLG | 5/8" - 3/4" |
| Knifty Knitter | Spool Loom | mauve/pink | plastic | - | 5 | XLG | 3/4" |
| Knifty Knitter | Spool Loom | mauve/pink | plastic | - | 8 | LG | 11/16" |
| Knifty Knitter | Flower loom | peach | plastic | - | 12 | XLG | 3/4" |
| Knifty Knitter | Small Round Loom | blue | plastic | - | 24 | LG | 5/8" |
| Knifty Knitter | Medium Round Loom | red | plastic | - | 31 | LG | 11/16" |
| Knifty Knitter | Large Round Loom | green | plastic | - | 36 | XLG | 3/4" |
| Knifty Knitter | Extra Large Round Loom | yellow | plastic | - | 41 | XLG | 13/16" |
| Knifty Knitter | Adult Hat Loom | purple | plastic | - | 48 | LG | 5/8" |
| Knifty Knitter (Mommy & Me) | Round Loom | maroon | plastic | - | 48 | LG | 5/8" |
| Knifty Knitter (Mommy & Me) | Round Loom | dark green | plastic | - | 31 | LG | 11/16" |
| Knifty Knitter | Long Loom | purple | plastic | 18 | 18 | XLG | 3/4" |
| Knifty Knitter | Long Loom | pink | plastic | 12 | 26 | LG | 11/16" |
| Knifty Knitter | Long Loom | yellow | plastic | 18 | 38 | LG | 11/16" |
| Knifty Knitter | Long Loom | green | plastic | 24 | 50 | LG | 11/16" |
| Knifty Knitter | Long Loom | blue | plastic | 30 | 63 | LG | 11/16" |

*Kiss Looms are adjustable by number of pegs used in the round as well as gauge adjustable and mimic the needle sizes in needle knitting by allowing you to add washers between the peg and pin boards to change the gauge of the fabric produced. With a single loom you can knit patterns from a size 7 to a size 13 needle or a 3/8" to 3/4" loom pattern. Washers can be added in any increment.*

**Modular looms (from Kiss) are made to connect together to make any size loom with any peg count;*
*1 End Pair set and Peg Sides (the longest side of the loom; bought as a pair) make up 1 loom. End Pairs peg count options vary per loom.*

| Needle Range | C2C | Gauge |
|---|---|---|
| 1 - 3 (2.25 mm/3.25 mm) | 3/16" | EFG |
| 3 - 6 (3.25 mm/4 mm) | 1/4" | FG |
| 5 - 8 (3.75 mm/5 mm) | 5/16", 3/8", 7/16" | SG |
| 8 - 10 (5 mm/6 mm) | 1/2", 9/16" | RG |
| 10 - 13 (6 mm/9 mm) | 5/8", 11/16" | LG |
| 13 - 15 (9 mm/10 mm) | 3/4", 13/16", 7/8", 15/16" | XLG |
| 19 - 35 (12.75 mm/20+) | +/- 1 1/2" | JUMBO |

| Yarn Weight Range (UK/AU) | Average sts per in | Crochet (US) |
|---|---|---|
| US 0 - 2 ( 1-3 ply) | 7 - 9 sts | A - D |
| US 1 - 3 (2-4 ply & 8 ply) | 5 - 7 sts | D - G |
| US 2 - 4 ( 2-4 ply, 8 ply & DK) | 4 - 5 sts | F - H |
| US 4 - 5 ( 8 - 12 ply, DK, Aran) | 3 - 4 sts | H - J |
| US 5 - 6 ( 10 - 12 ply, Aran, Chk) | 2 - 3 sts | J - M |
| US 6 - 7 ( 12 ply & Chunky) | 1.5 - 3 sts | M - N+ |
| US 6 - 7 ( Chunky & Roving) | .75 - 1 sts | M - Q+ |

EFG=Extra Fine Gauge I FG=Fine Gauge I SG=Small Gauge I RG=Regular Gauge I LG=Large Gauge I XLG=Extra Large Gauge I JUMBO=Extra Large Gauge+

## Loom Gauge Chart

| Brand | Loom Name/Type | Color | Peg | Pairs | Pegs | Gauge | C2C |
|---|---|---|---|---|---|---|---|
| Knitting Board (Size Adj only) | Hat Loom (using all pegs - SG) | white | plastic | - | 56-84 | SG | 3/8" |
| Knitting Board (Size Adj only) | Hat Loom (every other peg - XLG) | white | plastic | - | 28-42 | XLG | 3/4" |
| Knitting Board | Basics Loom (from Kit) | wood | plastic | 14 | 32 | SG | 7/16" |
| Knitting Board (Slide Adj Size) | 18" AllnOne Loom w/ 5 peg ext. | wood | plastic | 48 | 16-106 | SG | 3/8" |
| Knitting Board (Bolt Adj size) | 18" AllnOne Loom w/ 20 peg ext. | wood | plastic | 48 | 64, 88, 112, 136 | SG | 3/8" |
| Knitting Board (Bolt Adj size) | 28" Afghan Loom w/ 20 peg ext. | wood | plastic | 64 | 72, 104, 136, 168 | SG | 7/16" |
| Knitting Board (Slide Adj Size) | 28" Afghan Loom w/ 6 peg ext. | wood | plastic | 64 | 18- 140 | SG | 7/16" |
| Knitting Board | Tadpole Knitting Board | wood | metal pin | 16 | 32 | SG | 5/16" |
| Knitting Board | 10" Small Gauge Knitting Board | wood | metal pin | 22 | 44 | SG | 5/16" |
| Knitting Board | 28" Small Gauge Knitting Board | wood | metal pin | 84 | 168 | SG | 5/16" |
| Knitting Board | 38" Afghan Knitting Board | wood | metal pin | 112 | 224 | SG | 5/16" |
| Knitting Board | Adult Sock Loom (1 size) | white | metal | - | 52 | FG | 1/4" |
| Knitting Board (Size Adj only) | Sock Loom original | white | metal | - | 16-60 | FG | 1/4" |
| Knitting Board (Size Adj only) | Sock Loom 2 | white | plastic | - | 16-54 | SG | 3/8" |
| Knitting Board (Size Adj only) | Sock Loom EFG | white | plastic | - | 24-112 | EFG | 3/16" |
| Knitting Board - "S" shape | Super Afghan Loom ("S") | white | plastic | 77 | 198 | SG | 7/16" |
| Knitting Board - ZIPPY | ZIPPY (opt, corners w/pegs avail) | yellow | plastic | - | 4+ w/ connectors | XLG - JUMBO | 1 1/2" |
| Knitting Frame Noble Knitter | 19" Oak Knitting Board | oak | cotter pin | 48 | 96 | SG | 1/3" |
| Knitting Frame Noble Knitter | 34" Oak Knitting Board | oak | cotter pin | 92 | 184 | SG | 1/3" |
| Knitting Frame Noble Knitter | Noble Knitter 25 | plastic | cotter pin | 25 | 50 | SG | 1/3" |
| Knitting Frame Noble Knitter | Noble Knitter 50 | plastic | cotter pin | 50 | 100 | SG | 1/3" |
| Knitting Frame Noble Knitter | Noble Knitter 100 | plastic | cotter pin | 100 | 200 | SG | 1/3" |
| Loops & Threads | Small Round Loom | bright blue | plastic | - | 24 | LG | 5/8" |
| Loops & Threads | Medium Round Loom | purple | plastic | - | 31 | LG | 11/16" |
| Loops & Threads | Large Round Loom | orange | plastic | - | 36 | XLG | 3/4" |
| Loops & Threads | Extra Large Round Loom | bright pink | plastic | - | 41 | XLG | 13/16" |
| Lion Brand (Adj size & 2+gauges) | Martha Stewart Loom/Weave (SG) | plastic | plastic | 7-79 | 24 to 200 | SG | 3/8" |
| Lion Brand (Adj size & 2+gauges) | Martha Stewart Loom/Weave (XLG) | plastic | plastic | 4-40 | 12 to 100 | XLG | 3/4" |

GUIDE: Use Chart to convert needle patterns to best loom & yarn. Look at stitches per inch and needle size. Test the yarn on your loom with a gauge swatch. Adjust yarn to thinner for more sts per in or thicker for less. Wash or block swatch before measuring for accuaracy.

(Sts per in low range is lowest sts per inch with smallest recommended needle. Higher sts per in. is for larger needle. The same applies to Yarn Weight)

US Yarn Weight chart: 0="Lace"-Fingering/10-CT Crochet thread  1="Super Fine"-Sock, Fingering, Baby  2="Fine"-Sport, Bab  3="Light"-DK, Light Worsted  4="Medium"-Worsted, Afghan, Aranl  5="Bulky"-Chunky, Craft, Rug  6="Super Bulky"-Bulky, Roving  7="Jumbo"-Jumbo, Roving

| Needle Range | C2C | Gauge |
|---|---|---|
| 1 - 3 (2.25 mm/3.25 mm) | 3/16" | EFG |
| 3 - 6 (3.25 mm/4 mm) | 1/4" | FG |
| 5 - 8 (3.75 mm/5 mm) | 5/16", 3/8", 7/16" | SG |
| 8 - 10 (5 mm/6 mm) | 1/2", 9/16" | RG |
| 10 - 13 (6 mm/9 mm) | 5/8", 11/16" | LG |
| 13 - 15 (9 mm/10 mm) | 3/4", 13/16", 7/8", 15/16" | XLG |
| 19 - 35 (12.75 mm/20+) | +/- 1 1/2" | JUMBO |

| Yarn Weight Range (UK/AU) | Average sts per in | Crochet (US) |
|---|---|---|
| US 0 - 2 ( 1-3 ply) | 7 - 8 sts | A - D |
| US 1 - 3 ( 2-4 ply & 8 ply) | 5 - 7 sts | D - G |
| US 2 - 4 ( 2-4 ply, 8 ply & DK) | 4 - 5 sts | F - H |
| US 4 - 5 ( 8 - 12 ply, DK, Aran) | 3 - 4 sts | H - J |
| US 5 - 6 ( 10 - 12 ply, Aran, Chk) | 2 - 3 sts | J - M |
| US 6 - 7 ( 12 ply & Chunky) | 1.5 - 3 sts | M - N+ |
| US 6 - 7 ( Chunky & Roving) | .75 - 1 sts | M - Q+ |

**EFG=Extra Fine Gauge I FG=Fine Gauge I SG=Small Gauge I RG=Regular Gauge I LG=Large Gauge I XLG=Extra Large Gauge I JUMBO=Extra Large Gauge+**
**Chart Copyright 2015 GoodKnit Kisses; for personal use. *Not an exhaustive list; contact if errors; not all Brands are still in production.**

### Swatch Math: How many Stitches to Cast-on? How many Rows to knit?

Tip - wash or block item first; most gauges called out in patterns are blocked first before measuring.

#### Cast-On Formula used:

Swatch is S stitches and measures W wide. The stitches per inch is S/W and desired width is dW.

The Stitches to Cast-On = (dW x S/W). Divide Stitches counted in swatch by swatch Width measured. Multiply by Desired Width.

#### Now for the Rows Calculations:

Formula for rows needed = (dL x R/L) where dL is desired length, R is number of measured rows and L is length measured.

Divide Rows counted in swatch by swatch Length measured. Multiply by Desired Length.

# Chapter 5

In this chapter we'll explore some of the basic math you can use to create more knitting projects as you explore and grow in skills. Don't be afraid! You can do this.

It's true that if you use a pattern with the exact loom, the exact yarn and the exact stitch then you will get a finished item that is very close to the original design. You CAN make lots of hats and scarves forever and never need to know the math. However, sometimes you may want the item bigger, need a specific size, want to change the main stitch pattern, or try a new design all on your own. The following sections should help.

Use this chapter for reference, as we will cover:
1. Why Swatch? – What is a swatch? Why make one? And "Making a Gauge Swatch"
2. Measure Knitting Gauge - measure a gauge swatch for knitting gauge
3. Cast-on Calculator – determine stitches to cast-on for width
4. Row Calculator – determine rows to knit for desired length
5. Yarn Required – determine the yards (or meters) needed or used for a project
6. Magic Circle Formula – create a circle
7. Sock Math – make socks of all sizes

## Why Swatch?
*What is a swatch?*
A swatch is a small sample of knitting that represents the main stitch pattern for your pattern. A swatch is used for knitting with needles, on a loom, or crochet.

*Why make a swatch?*
A gauge swatch can also show what the repeated pattern will look like in the chosen yarn. If you do have a large stitch pattern, make sure it is a full repeat or if smaller be sure to knit at least 3 repeats. Most importantly, making a swatch helps determine "gauge" or stitches needed to tweak a pattern for size, tools or yarn.

## Making a Gauge Swatch
To begin, knit a 6"x6" flat panel and bind off your swatch. Cast on 10 more stitches than is listed in the pattern gauge when in doubt. Block your swatch for accuracy; this will represent what the swatch will look after it is cleaned and for lace it opens the stitches (see **Blocking**). If you are making an item that may only get spot cleaned you may choose not to block.

For reference write down the following and attach it to the swatch:
1. Loom used (Brand, Loom Name and other important information)
2. Yarn (Brand, style name, color name, weight class ex #4 worsted)
3. Stitch or stitch pattern used and how many stitches casted on (note if slip stitch is used); now keep it all on file. Go one step further and measure your swatch then file that with the swatch or keep a record for yourself on a spreadsheet. (see **Measure Knitting Gauge** below)
4. Note if swatch was blocked or not blocked.

Measuring a gauge swatch or your work in progress

Fast-forwarded to video lesson on gauge.

130            131

**Measure Knitting Gauge**

Measure the swatch[132]; refer to the notes and illustrations below for help. Using a hard ruler or swatch ruler, measure and count how many stitches are in a 4 inch (or 10 cm) wide area and then how many rows are in a 4 inch (or 10 cm) length area. For best results measure 1" away from the sides and ends of your 6" x 6" (15 x 15 cm) swatch. These numbers will determine a full picture of the final gauge achieved. Write down your results. Stitches counted across the row are "stitches per inch (cm)" and down the length are "rows per inch (or cm)". This is the swatch-measured knitting gauge; see numbered list for details on how to note your gauge.

**TIP!** Use small DPNs (double pointed needles) or round toothpicks to mark the first and last stitches to make counting easier [see photo].

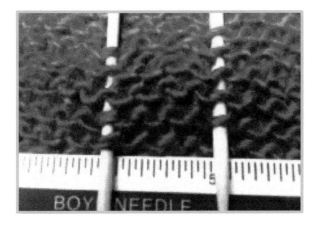

1. Write the number of stitches counted in the measurement.
2. Next write the width measured when you counted the stitches across the row. If you counted 12 stitches in a 4 in (10 cm) row then your note will say 12 sts per 4 in (10 cm). For U.S. knitters divide by 4 for "sts per 1 in". To continue the above example: 4 sts per 1 in = 12 sts per 4 in.
3. Next write the length measured when you counted the stitches down a column of rows/ length of the swatch.
4. Last notes to write; if you counted 20 rows in 4 inches (10 cm), then your note will say 20 rows per 4 in (10 cm). For U.S. knitters divide by 4 for rows per in. To continue the above example: 5 rows per 1 in = 20 rows per 4 in.

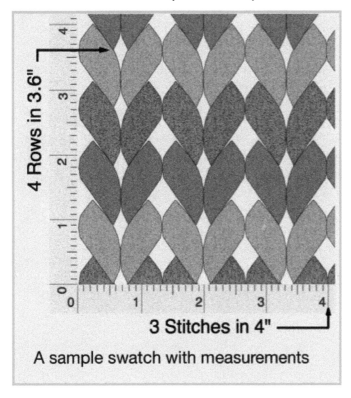

A sample swatch with measurements

You now know your swatch-**measured knitting gauge!**

## Obtaining Pattern Gauge – Help, my gauge is off!

To find your pattern gauge it only takes a few simple calculations after you know the swatch-measured gauge. If you simply want to find how many stitches you need for a panel, or even a small section to make a feature in your knitting (ex. a special stitch or a 6" bound off slit for a strap to fit through), you will need to know how many stitches to work, bind-off to decrease or cast-on to increase. If you have the "stitches per inch" or "rows per inch" from an existing pattern, you can compare those numbers to your **measured knitting gauge** numbers and calculate the difference needed. Then add or subtract stitches to achieve the same sizing or also the same as "obtain(ing) gauge". Use the calculators (math formulas) below for help.

*Note that gauge can change slightly with your own mood and tension as well as from yarn to yarn even on the same tools. *

## Calculator General Notes:

The first examples contain numbers to help you practice. We encourage you to use the formula spelled out, along with the example numbers in the example photos, to test our answers. Below the examples are cleared out boxes for you to use as a guide for your own swatch measurements.

**(A note for our **metric** friendly international users. The calculations will work the same; just change inches to suit your needs. It's the ratio that's important). **

**TIP!** If your desired width is a circumference for a snug fit, an adjustment to the number to enter may be needed. For example, on socks measure around the widest part of foot snugly and subtract 1/2 inch; now write this as the new desired width.

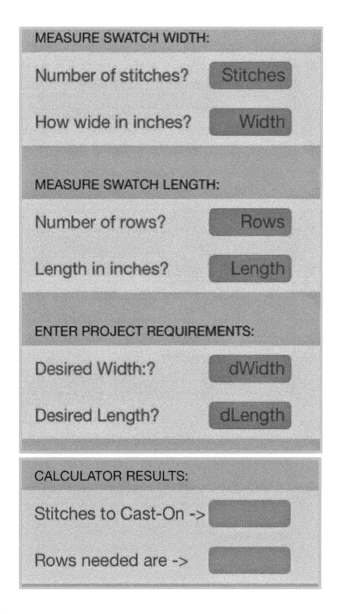

**MEASURE SWATCH WIDTH:**

Number of stitches? `Stitches`

How wide in inches? `Width`

**MEASURE SWATCH LENGTH:**

Number of rows? `Rows`

Length in inches? `Length`

**ENTER PROJECT REQUIREMENTS:**

Desired Width:? `dWidth`

Desired Length? `dLength`

**CALCULATOR RESULTS:**

Stitches to Cast-On ->

Rows needed are ->

**Cast-On Formula:**

Swatch is "S" stitches and measures "W" wide. The stitches per inch are S/W and desired width is "dW". The Stitches to Cast-On = (dW x S/W). Divide Stitches counted in swatch-by-swatch Width measured. Multiply by Desired Width.

So for the example for the below you will:
1. Look at your 4 x 4 measured area.
2. Write the stitches down in that area; which is 20.
3. Your desired width is for 8" (inches).
4. So your math will take 20 (S) divided by 4 (W); now multiply by 8 (dW or desired width) = Result is to cast-on 40 stitches.

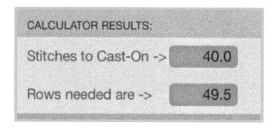

**MEASURE SWATCH WIDTH:**

Number of stitches?  20

How wide in inches?  4

**MEASURE SWATCH LENGTH:**

Number of rows?  11

Length in inches?  4

**ENTER PROJECT REQUIREMENTS:**

Desired Width:?  8

Desired Length?  18

**CALCULATOR RESULTS:**

Stitches to Cast-On ->  40.0

Rows needed are ->  49.5

**Row Formula:**
Formula for rows needed = (dL x R/L) where "dL" is desired length, "R" is number of measured rows and "L" is length measured.
Ex. Divide Rows counted on the swatch by Length measured.  Multiply by Desired Length.

So for the example for the below you will:
1. Look at your 4 x 4 measured area.
2. Write the rows down the length; which is 11
3. Your desired length is for 18" (inches).
4. So your math will take 11 (R) divided by 4 (L); now multiply by 18  (dW or desired length) = Result is to knit 49-50 rows to have 18 inches.

## MEASURE SWATCH WIDTH:

| | |
|---|---|
| Number of stitches? | 20 |
| How wide in inches? | 4 |

## MEASURE SWATCH LENGTH:

| | |
|---|---|
| Number of rows? | 11 |
| Length in inches? | 4 |

## ENTER PROJECT REQUIREMENTS:

| | |
|---|---|
| Desired Width:? | 8 |
| Desired Length? | 18 |

## CALCULATOR RESULTS:

| | |
|---|---|
| Stitches to Cast-On -> | 40.0 |
| Rows needed are -> | 49.5 |

**Yarn Required Calculator:**

If you learn to calculate yarn used in project gives you benefits!:

- Find out how much you **used** for your small knit item to tell someone, make more, or write a pattern.
- Find out how much yarn is **left** on a ball. This could be used to make a matching pair to a sock or glove or even make a matching hat after you've made a scarf!
- Find out how many balls or skeins of yarn you need to make your blanket or large project.

**Supplies - To calculate yarn you will need the following:**
1. Have your knitting project or knitted gauge swatch and the remaining yarn. *(TIP: To estimate yarn needed, have notes ready from your pattern for the desired overall size and measured knitted gauge notes.)*
2. Gram scale. I recommend purchasing an inexpensive gram scale that can switch between ounces and grams. Personally I use grams for weighing because it seems to be the most precise. I got my scale at a local office supply store for under $25 USD. *(TIP: In a pinch you can take your knitting to your local postal service to be weighed in a common area with a public scale.)*
3. Label - Ball band or wrapper from yarn for information. *(TIP: You can also look up this information on the manufacturer's website or a site that sells the yarn you used if the ball band is lost.)*
4. Calculator
5. Pencil & paper; or note on your electronic device.

Let's figure out **how much yarn** you need for you project or check the math for something you have recently made to help confirm the following numbers. For a video explanation, along with a basic yarn class, visit the link below.

**How Much Yarn Was Used? Formula:**
1. Read the label and write the number of grams. Example 100 grams (g).
2. Weigh item on gram scale and write down. Example 45 g for my 2 fingerless mitts. *TIP: If the item is too wide you can place a bowl on the scale before turning the scale on to offset the weight. The bowl will now hold your item and weigh accurate. If your knitting is just too large then weigh the leftover yarn to calculate what amount remains and take that number from how many balls were used.*
3. Read the label and write the number of yards (meters). Even if you use yards it still works to measure in grams instead of ounces. I like to measure in grams. Example 128 yards = "y" (117 meters).
4. Take yarn total "y" (yards) divided by yarn total "g" (grams) = ypg (yards per gram) for that entire ball of yarn. *TIP: For metric use "m" or meters instead of "y".*
5. For example if my mitts used a yarn that is 128 y I divide that by 100 g for the yarn weight. My ypg is 1.28. *(For metric 117 m / 100 g = 1.17 mpg).*
6. Next use this formula to determine amount used. g (of item) x ypg = yards used (or meters in metric).
7. For example 45 g x 1.28 ypg = 57.5 yds used. *(For metric 45 g x 1.17 mpg = 52.65 m).*
8. This means I can also see what **remains on the ball** by taking the original yardage minus the yards used. *TIP: If possible, weigh item and remaining ball (with wrapper on) to verify the starting weight.*
9. For example the ball had 128 yards – 57.5 yards for mitts = approximately 70.5 yards left (64.35 meters). I could make another set of mitts!

Now that you know how to calculate the yarn from a finished project, you can use that information to estimate the yards needed from a swatch.

**How Much Yarn Do I Need To Buy? Formula:**

1. Weigh your measured swatch on the gram scale following the **yarn used formula** above following steps 1 - 8. Write that down as yards used. Practice Example: Your 6 x 6 in (15 cm x 15 cm) swatch is 15 grams. And your yarn used end up as 19.2 yards (17.55 m) for a 6 x 6 in (15 cm x 15 cm) area.
2. Write down the overall size of the knitting; round up to the nearest whole number. For example a 55 1/2 x 60 in would be 56 x 60 in (141 cm x 153 cm). *TIP: If it is an odd shaped piece, measure in rectangles or squares to cover the area. With this method, you may have a few or just cover as one large square or rectangle. You will estimate more yarn than needed but will have enough.*
3. Calculate the square inches (or square cm) of the *desired knitting* area(s). Example 56 x 60 in = 3360 sq in (21,573 sq cm).
4. Calculate the square inches (or square cm) of the *swatch knitting* area. Example 6 x 6 in = 36 sq in (225 sq cm).
5. Calculate desired knitting sq in (or cm) divided by swatch knitting sq in (or cm). Example 3,360 / 36 = 93.333 (or metric 21,573 sq cm / 225 sq cm = 95.88)
6. Multiple that result times the yards (meters) for the swatch area. Example 93.333 x 19.2 yds = 1,792 yds. (Or metric 95.88 x 17.55 meters = 1,682.69 meters).
7. Divide that number by the quantity in the original ball of yarn. Example 1,792 yds (1,683 meters) / 128 yds (117 meters) = 13.99 (14.38) balls or 15 balls of yarn. Buy 16-17 for incidentals; make sure they are all the same dye lot.

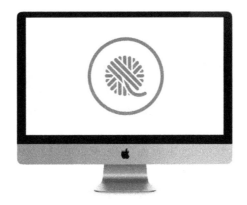

Yarn Class 101- Yarn
Lingo & estimate

Now you can estimate how much yarn you need[133]. Let's shop, yay!!!

Towards the end of this chapter you will see Charts to help you figure out general sizes to knit for blankets, hats, socks and body measurements for babies, children, men and women. Included with the charts are some tips along the way.

This next section, on the Magic Circle Formula, is much more advanced math & knitting but I'm including it for reference.

**Magic Circle Formula**
The Magic Formula to make any size flat circle.
In our <u>knitting and crochet craft club on Facebook</u>[134] I've had the pleasure to meet many people of all walks of life virtually. Meet Joann Fernstrom. Many years ago she became friends with a lady named Alles Hutchinson. Alles published a wonderful educational magazine (booklet) called NEWS & VIEWS put out by ALLES KNITTING PUBLICATIONS from Pittsburgh, PA. She wrote and taught about machine knitting especially. She had a Magic Formula for knitting any size circle to make hats, shawls, afghans and the like. You can apply it to many things. Before she passed Alles gave her friend Joann the formula to help others. In an effort to get this out there, for her dear friend, Joann has asked me to share it with you today. Alles wrote many patterns and charts for machine knitting and can be used on looms. I urge you to check out those older publications as well! Here is a word from Joann in her voice.

"I have seen some of you [the group] asking how to figure out how to make a circle. I have a formula for doing this any size you would like. It is called the magic formula and you can figure out whatever size you want your circle to be as long as you have a long enough loom. When you make a flat circle blanket you must determine the size of a circle to make then how many panels you want then after a few figures. The Magic Formula was figured out by a very dear friend [Alles] who passed away about 30 years ago and she gave it to me to share as I pleased."- Joann Fernstrom

$$\frac{2}{25 \text{ rows} \ / \ 50 \text{ stitches}}$$
$$50$$

# CIRCLE MAGIC FORMULA ("CORRECTED")
## by Alles Hutchinson[135]
Magic Formula for Circles by Alles Hutchinson[136]

## CIRCULAR SHAWL OR AFGHAN

This is Magic Formula offered to you so that you can learn the way to figure out making short rows. Once you learn this formula you will be able to make hats, shawls or Afghans [using short rows or "wrap & turns"] .

The entire piece is done by short rows (partial knitting). You will need only one measurement— how wide do you want the finish piece to be.
For example we will use 2.25 stitches and 4 rows = 1 inch. The diameter will be 40 inches. With 10 panels. You will substitute your own stitches and rows, and how many panels you want, but follow the same principle.

1. Find the circumference of the circle.
   FORMULA: to find the circumference of a circle, multiply the circumference of a circle,40 inch circle.
   40 x 3.14 (pie) = 125.6 (six is larger then 5 so the answer is 126)
2. Change inches to rows.
   126 x 4 rows per inch = 504 rows around the edge.
3. Decide how many panels you want:
   10 panels .....504 rows divided by 10 panels = 50.4 (4 is less then 5 so the answer is 50).
4. Find the radius of circle and change inches to stitches. Radius = 1⁄2 the diameter of the circle.
   40 inches divided by 2 = 20
   20 x 2 stitches per inch = 40 (this is what you will cast on).
5. Shape this by short rows so that it will become a pie shaped piece. Each section will be short rowed down to the next to the last group. The last group will not be worked. Then 2 rows are knitted over all needles. Since short rows are done only on alternate rows, divide the number of rows by 2. 50 rows divided by 2 = 25 rows.
6. Distribute the stitches evenly over these rows. You have 40 stitches to shape in 25 rows. Since the answer you want is stitches, divide rows into stitches.25 rows divided into 50 = 2 stitches to short row.

Therefore you will short row 2 stitches every other row.

So you will cast on 40 stitches and knit back but don't do peg 1 and 2. Lift stitch 2 off peg and wrap yarn on it. Replace stitch and knit back to peg 40 then knit to peg 5 and then back to peg 40. You will short row 2 stitches every other row when you get to the last 2 stitches you will knit over all the stitches.
Then change to 2nd color or keep it in one color. Remember there are no knitting police out there so let you imagination run wild and do as many colors as you prefer and as many panels as you want.

ANOTHER EXAMPLE:
Lets say your stitches were 7 stitches and 10 rows per inch and you wanted it 46-inch circle.

Using 10 panels.

Here is how you would do it.
- 46 inches x 3.14 (pi) = 144.44 = 144 using the 4 is lower then 5.
- 144 inches x 10 rows =1440 rows around the entire edge.
- Radius = 1⁄2 the diameter.
- 46 inch divided by 2 = 23 inches x 7 stitches per inch =161 stitches to cast on. Now shape the short rows.
- 144 divided by 2 =72 rows
- Now we have 161 stitches to shape in 72 rows.

Therefore you will short row 3 stitches 17 times then 2 sts ever other row 55 times.
Now to prove it 17+55= 72 rows
23 inches x 7 stitches = 161 stitches.
I hope you can understand this Magic Formula for flat circles.
– Alles (and Joann)

```
        sts     2   + 1 +  = 3 stitches
72 rows/  161 stitches
 -17        -144
55 times  17 times
```

Note from Kristen:
I have done the math using Lion Brand Hometown USA knitting gauge for size 13 needles.  Here is my math for a 36″ diameter circle across with 8 wedges (like a pie)
Pre-work:
- Gauge 9 sts (stitches) x 12 rows 4x4 swatch.  So that is 2.25 sts per in. x 3 rows per in.
- 36 in is the width (diameter) I want.
- 8 is the number of panels I want to knit up. Say I want to use 8 colors and change on every "panel" or wedge.

1. 36 dia x 3.14 (# for Pi) = 113.04 –> 113
2. 113 x 3 rows per in = 339 sts around edge
3. 339 / 8 panels = 42.375 –> 42 rows
4. 36 dia / 2 = 18 radius –> 18 rad. x 2.25 sts per in. = 40.5 –> 41 sts cast-on
5. Short rows will be every other row. Work these rows short. –> 42 rows / 2 = 21 rows shaped with short rows
6. Shape 41 sts over 21 rows every __ stitches on each row. 42 / 21 = 2 sts (so every even stitch will be wrapped for a short row)

The following would happen:
Cast on 41 pegs.  (The word "work" can function as a knit or a purl stitch; short rows are in groups of 2 here.)

Row 1: Work back to peg 3 and wrap peg 2
Row 2: Work to peg 41
Row 3: Work to peg 5 and wrap peg 4.
Even rows repeat Row 2.
Odd rows repeat working back to 1 peg before even peg higher than previous row. Wrap that even peg. Continue until 1 full group (of 2) is left empty. Will have +1 left in this example.
Work last remaining stitches to 41.
End of 1st "panel". Change color as desired.
Repeat 7 more panels.

Have fun making your own magic formula circles!

## How to Measure

The following charts list specific body measurements. Refer to the list below to describe how to measure. These standards are called out by the Craft Yarn Council; graphics and more can be found at www.YarnStandards.com. Always check a pattern if another method is described by the designer or publisher.

1. Chest/Bust —Measure around the fullest part of the chest/bust. Do not draw the tape too tightly.
2. Center Back Neck–to-Cuff—With arm slightly bent, measure from back base of neck across shoulder around bend of elbow to wrist.
3. Back Waist Length—Measure from the most prominent bone at base of neck to the natural waistline.
4. Cross Back—Measure from shoulder to shoulder.
5. Sleeve Length—With arm slightly bent, measure from armpit to cuff.
6. Upper Arm—Measure around the widest section of the upper arm located above the elbow.
7. Armhole Depth—Measure from the top outside edge of the shoulder down to the armpit.
8. Waist—Measure your waist at the smaller circumference of your natural waist, usually just above the belly button.
9. Hip—Measure at the widest part of your lower hip.
10. Head—For an accurate head measure, place a tape measure across the forehead and measure around the full circumference of the head. Keep the tape snug for accurate results.
11. Sock Measurements—The following measurements are for crew-style or dress socks, which usually come several inches above the ankle and below the calf.
12. Foot Circumference—To determine the foot circumference, measure around the widest part of your foot.
13. Sock Height—To determine the height of the sock, measure from where you start to turn for the heel shaping to the top of the sock.
14. Total Foot Length—To measure the total length of your foot, place a ruler or tape measure on the floor. Position the back of your heel at the beginning of the tape and the measure to your longest toe.

**Sock Math -** is necessary to have a nice fitted sock. Use the chart to help determine average measurements for socks for: Preemie, Newborn, Infant, Baby, Toddler, Child, Teen, Women, and Men. Then knit up a <u>swatch</u>[137] with the yarn you want to use in the main stitch pattern. Be sure to use the needles or loom intended. Knit a 3×3 in swatch and measure 2″ across. Divide that number by two for your "gauge" (see **Why Swatch**).

**Sock Math Formula:**
1. Measure around ball of foot (widest part near toes); foot resting on it's weight.
2. Multiply # of inches by the gauge. (Gauge will need to be determined from measuring a swatch made with intended yarn and tools).
3. Subtract 10 % of this number for "negative give" for fitted socks.
4. The result is the number of stitches to cast on in the stitch used in swatch.

Here is some sock math broken down to explain:
Example for my size US 12 women's feet or US men's 10. Yes. I'm really tall:
1. Measurement of ball of foot – 9.5″
2. Ball of foot times 1″ of measured gauge swatch – 9.5″ x 7 = 66.5
3. Result from #2 multiplied by reciprocal of 10% – 66.5 x .90 = 59.85
4. Round stitches to nearest whole number (usually even on looms) – Cast on 60 pegs.

Sock Chart (measurements)

| | | | Infant/ Child | | | | Adult | |
|---|---|---|---|---|---|---|---|---|
| | Premie | Baby | Baby | Baby | Toddler | Child | Woman | Man |
| | 5-7 lbs | 7-9 lbs | 3 mth - 6 mth | 6 - 12 mths | 12 mth - 4 yrs | 5 - 12 yrs | | |
| Foot Length (in.) | 3" - 3 1/2" | 3 1/4" - 3 3/4" | 4" - 4 1/2" | 4.25" – 4 1/2" | 4.5" - 5" | 6" - 8 1/2" | 8" - 11" | 10" - 12" |
| (cm.) | 7-9 cm | 9-10 cm | 10-12 cm | 12-13 cm | 13-15 cm | 16-21 cm | 20-27 cm | 25-36 cm |
| Shoe Size (Ball of Foot) US only; Find Shoe Size and see Ball of Foot # in parenthesis | | | | | | 4 (5) / 5 (5.25) / 6 (5.5) 7 (5.75) / 8 (6) / 9 (6.25) 10 (6.5) / 11 (6.75) / 12 (7) / 13 (7.25) | 5 (7.5) / 6 (7.75) / 7 (8.25) 8 (8.5) / 9 (8.75) / 10 (9) 11 (9.25) / 12 (9.5) | 6 (8.25) / 7 (8.5) / 8 (8.75) 9 (9.25) / 10 (9.5) / 11 (9.75) 12 (10) / 13 (10.25) / 14 (10.5) |
| Yarn Amount Loom Gauge order EFG/ FG/ SG/ RG or U.S. Needle 1-3/ 3-6/ 6-8/ 5-7/ 8-10 | | | | | Fingering 270 Sport 210 DK 200 Worsted 180 | Fingering 350 Sport 280 DK 250 Worsted 225 | Fingering 450 Sport 380 DK 350 Worsted 320 | Fingering 550 Sport 450 DK 400 Worsted 350 |

\* Sizes based upon averages. For accuracy always measure the foot. Measurements should be taken with full weight upon the foot/resting. Length measurement is taken from the back of the heel to the large toe. The width of the foot is measured in the widest place, usually around the ball of the foot. Measurement from the back of the heel vertically to intended cuff will indicate the height of the sock.
\* For a slipper sock use the widest width. For a snug fitted sock take 10% off for negative give (ease)
**EFG** = Extra Fine Gauge (3/16") = Equiv. Needle 1-3 (2.25 mm - 3.5 mm)
**FG** = Fine Gauge (1/4") = Equiv. Needle 3-6 (3.5 mm - 4 mm/4.25 mm)z
**SG** = Small Gauge (5/16", 3/8", 7/16") = Equiv. Needle 6-8 (4 mm/4.25 mm - 5 mm/5.25 mm
**ES or SG** = (5/16, 3/8") = Equiv. Needle 5-7 (3.75 mm - 4.75 mm)]
**RG** = Regular Gauge (1/2", 9/16") = Equiv. Needle 8-10 (5 mm/5.25 mm - 6 mm)
**LG** = Large Gauge (5/8", 11/16") = Equiv. Needle 10-13 (6mm - 9 mm)
**XLG** = Extra Large Gauge (3/4", 13/16", 7/8", 15/16") = Equiv. Needle 13-15 (9 mm - 10 mm)

| | MATH on socks for knitters: |
|---|---|
| 1 | Measure around ball of your foot (at widest part near toes) with foot resting on it's weight. |
| 2 | Multiply # of inches by the gauge. (gauge will need to be determined from measuring a swatch made with intended yarn and tools). |
| 3 | Subtract 10 % of this number for negative give for fitted socks. |
| 4 | The result is the number of stitches to cast on in stitch used in swatch. |

Needle and Loom Knitting Reference Chart by Kristen Mangus

# HAT CHART

Use the chart below to help determine average head measurements for making hat or beanies. These are average measurements. You may need to factor in easement if your stitch pattern is particularly very stretchy or not much stretch at all.

Brims can vary in style and size. 2"-3" extra is included in the numbers below for a brim to fold up on adult hats and 1" for newborns. For preemies and newborns we suggest keeping a brimless hat (letting the stockinette roll) to allow for a gentle fit for baby.

Common Suggested brim styles are:
- Brimless (sometimes called rolled; can be confused with hemmed)
- Hemmed (cast on edge is brought back up after brim length is doubled and added back onto needles; continue knitting in the round – also sometimes called rolled but "hemmed" is a more accurate way to describe to discourage confusion.)
- Garter (Alternate a full row of Knit followed by a full row of purl. Repeat until desired brim length is achieved)
- Rib or Ribbed (Alternating series of knits and purls evenly throughout row. For example a 1×1 rub would be knit 1, purl 1 and repeat. This works on a multiple of 2. For a multiple of 2 or 4 a 2×2 rib can be achieved; *knit 2, purl 2* and repeat between *,*. Also written as *k2, p2* rep bet *,*. Other rib brims can be made but depends on row stitch count.

Hat Chart

|   |   |   |   | Infant/Child |   |   |   |   | Adult |   |
|---|---|---|---|---|---|---|---|---|---|---|
|   |   | Premie | Baby | Baby | Baby | Toddler | Child | Teens | Woman | Man |
|   |   |   | Newborn | 3 mth - 6 mth | 6 - 12 mths | 12 mth - 3 yrs | 3 - 10 years | or Petite |   |   |
| 1 | Head Circumference (in.) | 7" - 13" | 13" - 14" | 14" - 17" | 16" - 19" | 18" - 20" | 19" - 20 1/2" | 20 1/2" - 22" | 20" - 22 1/2" | 23" - 24" |
|   | (cm.) | 18-33 | 33-36 | 36-43 | 41-48 | 46-48 | 48-51 | 53-56 | 56 | 58.4-61 |
| 2 | Hat Height (in.) | 3" - 5 1/2" | 5 1/2 - 6" | 6 1/2 - 7" | 7 1/2" | 8" | 8 1/2" | 9" - 10" | 11" | 11"-11 1/2" |
|   | (cm.) | 8 - 15 | 13-15 | 15-18 | 18 | 20 | 22 | 25 | 28 | 30.5 |

*2-3" extra is in above numbers for folding up a brim on adults; 1" for newborns. Adjust accordingly

## BLANKET SIZES CHART

Use this chart as a guide to average measurements for blankets and afghans. If you need to determine cast-on stitches or rows to knit please read **Obtaining Pattern Gauge** or **Cast-On Formula**. To see how much yarn you need please read **Yarn Required Formula**.

## Blanket Sizes

| | |
|---|---|
| Lovey (in.) | 10" x 10" |
| Security/ Cuddle (in.) | 14" x 17" |
| Stroller/ Baby (in.) | 30" x 35" |
| Receiving (in.) | 40" x 40" |
| Toddler (in.) | 42" x 52" |
| Swaddle (in.) | 47" x 47" |
| Crib (in.) | 45" x 60" |
| Throw (in.) | 52" x 60" |
| Twin (in.) | 66" x 90" |
| Double (in.) | 90"x108" |
| Queen (in.) | 90"x108" |
| King (in.) | 108"x108" |

*1 inch = 2.54 centimeters

## BABY SIZES CHART

Use this chart as a guide to average measurements for babies when making sweaters (jumpers) or other garments for the upper body.

## Baby Sizes (clothing)

| | Baby's size | 3 months | 6 months | 12 months | 18 months | 24 months |
|---|---|---|---|---|---|---|
| 1 | Chest (in.) | 16 | 17 | 18 | 19 | 20 |
| | (cm.) | 40.5 | 43 | 45.5 | 48 | 50.5 |
| 2 | Center Back | 10 1/2 | 11 1/2 | 12 1/2 | 14 | 18 |
| | Neck-to-Cuff | 26.5 | 29 | 31.5 | 35.5 | 45.5 |
| 3 | Back Waist | 6 | 7 | 7 1/2 | 8 | 8 1/2 |
| | Length | 15.5 | 17.5 | 19 | 20.5 | 21.5 |
| 4 | Cross Back | 7 1/4 | 7 3/4 | 8 1/4 | 8 1/2 | 8 3/4 |
| | (Shoulder to shoulder) | 18.5 | 19.5 | 21 | 21.5 | 22 |
| 5 | Sleeve Length | 6 | 6 1/2 | 7 1/2 | 8 | 8 1/2 |
| | to Underarm | 15.5 | 16.5 | 19 | 20.5 | 21.5 |

*Numbers are based upon actual measurements; Measure person garment is for to get the best results. Add ease or the item
will be very close fitting. For Very-close fit; use chart chest/bust measurement or less. For Close-fitting: 1-2" (2.5-5cm); Standard-fitting: 2-4" (5-10cm); Loose-fitting: 4-6" (10-15cm); Oversized: 6" (15cm or more).

**CHILD SIZES**

Use this chart to help determine average measurements for children's sweaters (jumpers) or other upper body garment.

MAKING A SCARF?

For scarves on children, they range from desired width [3"-6"; or child's hand-span/width or double for a cowl. Good rule is 4"] to the child's height for length. If you are able to measure the person, I've found the best minimum scarf length should be from the chin to the floor when standing.  This allows the scarf to be hung long equally around the neck and fall in a "normal" way on a person.  Adjust accordingly if a much shorter design is requested or an extra long is required to double or triple the wraps around the neck of fashion.

For kid's keyhole scarves measure the circumference of their neck and add 16-18".  Knit 6-7" then start the hole and work till it's the right length (about 2").  Now finish the length of the scarf.  The keyhole scarf uses less yarn but more importantly keeps the scarf on the child and tucks into jackets better.

## Child Sizes (clothing)

| | Child's size | 2 | 4 | 6 | 8 | 10 | 12 | 14 | 16 |
|---|---|---|---|---|---|---|---|---|---|
| 1 | Chest (in.) | 21 | 23 | 25 | 26 1/2 | 28 | 30 | 31 1/2 | 32 1/2 |
| | (cm.) | 53 | 58.5 | 63.5 | 67 | 71 | 76 | 80 | 82.5 |
| 2 | Center Back | 18 | 19 1/2 | 20 1/2 | 22 | 24 | 26 | 27 | 28 |
| | Neck-to-Cuff | 45.5 | 49.5 | 52 | 56 | 61 | 66 | 68.5 | 71 |
| 3 | Back Waist | 8 1/2 | 9 1/2 | 10 1/2 | 12 1/2 | 14 | 15 | 15 1/2 | 16 |
| | Length | 21.5 | 24 | 26.5 | 31.5 | 35.5 | 38 | 39.5 | 40.5 |
| 4 | Cross Back | 9 1/4 | 9 3/4 | 10 1/4 | 10 3/4 | 11 1/4 | 12 | 12 1/4 | 13 |
| | (Shoulder to shoulder) | 23.5 | 25 | 26 | 27 | 28.5 | 30.5 | 31 | 33 |
| 5 | Sleeve Length | 8 1/2 | 10 1/2 | 11 1/2 | 12 1/2 | 13 1/2 | 15 | 16 | 16 1/2 |
| | to Underarm | 21.5 | 26.5 | 29 | 31.5 | 34.5 | 38 | 40.5 | 42 |

*Numbers are based upon actual measurements; Measure person garment is for to get the best results. Add ease or the item will be very close fitting. Very-close fit; use chart chest/bust measurement or less. For Close-fitting: 1-2" (2.5-5cm); Standard-fitting: 2-4" (5-10cm); Loose-fitting: 4-6" (10-15cm); Oversized: 6" (15cm or more).

## WOMEN SIZES FOR CLOTHING
Chart for Women sizes to help calculate stitches and rows for knitting and crochet.

Use this chart to help determine average measurements for women sizes for sweaters & (jumpers) & cardigans or other upper body garment.

MAKING A SCARF?

For scarves on women, they range from desired width (6″-8″; Yours can be skinnier or wider) to 60″ in length but that generally is too short for some or too long for others due to our beautiful variety of women's heights and body types. If you are able to measure the person, I've found the best minimum scarf length should be from the chin to the floor when standing (or for winter the person's height). This allows the scarf to be hung long equally around the neck and fall in a "normal" way on a person. Adjust accordingly if a much shorter design is requested (36″ to tuck into jacket) or an extra long is required to double or triple the wraps around the neck of fashion. **If the person is a plus size the size may need extra length (3″-12″) to accommodate or scarf will appear too short.**

## WOMEN SIZES CHART
The Women Sizes Chart numbers are based upon actual measurements; Measure person garment is to get the best results. Add ease or the item will be very close fitting. For Very-close fit; use chart chest/bust measurement or less. For Close-fitting: 1-2″ (2.5-5cm); Standard-fitting: 2-4″ (5-10cm); Loose-fitting: 4-6″ (10-15cm); Oversized: 6″ (15cm or more).

# Women Sizes (clothing)

| | Size | X-Small | Small | Medium | Large | 1X | 2X | 3X | 4X | 5X |
|---|---|---|---|---|---|---|---|---|---|---|
| 1 | Bust (in.) | 28" – 30" | 32" – 34" | 36" – 38" | 40" – 42" | 44" – 46" | 48" – 50" | 52" – 54" | 56" – 58" | 60" – 62" |
| | (cm.) | 71 – 76 | 81 – 86 | 91.5 – 96.5 | 101.5 – 106.5 | 111.5 – 117 | 122 – 127 | 132 – 137 | 142 – 147 | 152 – 158 |
| 2 | Center Back | 27" – 27.5" | 28" – 28.5" | 29" – 29.5" | 30" – 30.5" | 31" – 31.5" | 31.5" – 32" | 32.5" – 33" | 32.5" - 33" | 33" – 33.5" |
| | Neck-to-Cuff | 68.5 – 70 | 71 – 72.5 | 73.5 – 75 | 76 – 77.5 | 78.5 – 80 | 80 – 81.5 | 82.5 – 84 | 82.5 – 84 | 84 – 85 |
| 3 | Back Waist | 16.5" | 17" | 17.25" | 17.5" | 17.75" | 18" | 18" | 18.5" | 18.5" |
| | Length | 42 | 43 | 43.5 | 44.5 | 45 | 45.5 | 45.5 | 47 | 47 |
| 4 | Cross Back | 14" – 14.5" | 14.5" – 15" | 16" – 16.5" | 17" – 17.5" | 17.5" | 18" | 18" | 18.5" | 18.5" |
| | (Shoulder to Shoulder) | 35.5 – 37 | 37 – 38 | 40.5 – 42 | 43 – 44.5 | 44.5 | 45.5 | 45.5 | 47 | 47 |
| 5 | Sleeve Length | 16.5" | 17" | 17" | 17.5" | 17.5" | 18" | 18" | 18 .5" | 18.5" |
| | to Underarm | 42 | 43 | 43 | 44.5 | 44.5 | 45.5 | 45.5 | 47 | 47 |

*Numbers are based upon actual measurements; Measure person for to get best results. Add ease or the item will be very close fitting. For Very-close fit; use chart chest/bust measurement or less. Close-fitting: 1-2" (2.5-5 cm); Standard-fitting: 2-4" (5-10 cm); Loose-fitting: 4-6" (10-15 cm); Oversized: 6" (15 cm or more).

**MEN SIZES CHART**
Use this Men Sizes Chart to help determine average measurements for men's sweaters (jumpers) or other upper body garment.

MAKING A SCARF?

For scarves on men, they range from desired width (3"-7") to 60"-72" in length. If you are able to measure the person, I've found the best minimum scarf length should be from the chin to the floor when standing. This allows the scarf to be hung long equally around the neck and fall in a "normal" way on a person. Adjust accordingly if a much shorter design is requested or an extra long is required to double or triple the wraps around the neck of fashion.

The Men Sizes Chart numbers are based upon actual measurements; Measure person garment is to get the best results. Add ease or the item will be very close fitting. For Very-close fit; use chart chest/bust measurement or less. For Close-fitting: 1-2" (2.5-5cm); Standard-fitting: 2-4" (5-10cm); Loose-fitting: 4-6" (10-15cm); Oversized: 6" (15cm or more).

## Men Sizes (clothing)

| | Size | Small | Medium | Large | X-Large | XX-Large |
|---|---|---|---|---|---|---|
| 1 | Chest (in.) | 34" – 36" | 38" – 40" | 42" – 44" | 46" – 48" | 50" – 52" |
| | (cm.) | 86 – 91.5 | 96.5 – 101.5 | 106.5 – 111.5 | 116.5 – 122 | 127 – 132 |
| 2 | Center Back | 32" – 32.5" | 33" – 33.5" | 34" – 34.5" | 35" – 35.5" | 36" – 36.5" |
| | Neck-to-Cuff | 81 – 82.5 | 83.5 – 85 | 86.5 – 87.5 | 89 – 90 | 91.5 – 92.5 |
| 3 | Back Hip | 25" – 25.5" | 26.5" – 26.75" | 27" – 27.25" | 27.5" – 27.75" | 28" – 28.5" |
| | Length | 63.5 – 64.5 | 67.5 – 68 | 68.5 – 69 | 69.5 – 70.5 | 71 – 72.5 |
| 4 | Cross Back | 15.5" – 16" | 16.5" – 17" | 17.5" – 18" | 18" – 18.5" | 18.5" – 19" |
| | (Shoulder to Shoulder) | 39.5 – 40.5 | 42 – 43 | 44.5 – 45.5 | 45.5 – 47 | 47 – 48 |
| 5 | Sleeve Length | 18" | 18.5" | 19.5" | 20" | 20.5" |
| | to Underarm | 45.5 | 47 | 49.5 | 50.5 | 52 |

*Numbers are based upon actual measurements; Measure person garment is for to get the best results. Add ease or the item will be very close fitting. Very-close fit; use chart chest/bust measurement or less. For Close-fitting: 1-2" (2.5-5cm); Standard-fitting: 2-4" (5-10cm); Loose-fitting: 4-6" (10-15cm); Oversized: 6" (15cm or more).

# Patterns

# Flower Wrap Bracelet or Necklace

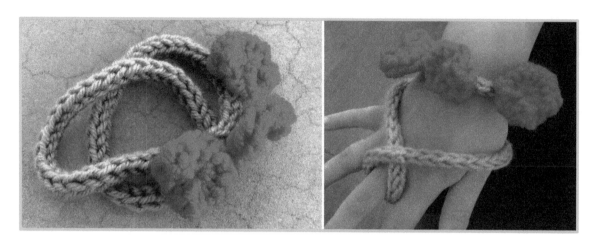

This cute wrap bracelet can be wrapped on your wrist a few times or even worn as a necklace or headband. Make for yourself or a friend!

Beginner / Débutant / Novicecia

**Stitches and Special Techniques Used In This Project:** SlipKnot
E-Wrap Cast-On
Gathered Bind-Off

**Materials:**
Color A – Main bracelet color. Approximately 12 yds #4 worsted weight yarn. (Original sample in green)
Color B – Flower color. Approximately 3 yds each flower or 9 yds for 3 flowers. #4 worsted weight yarn. (Original sample in pink)

**Loom and Yarn Needle:**
16 peg 5/8" gauge loom from CinDWood or 12 peg XLG Flower Loom or similar. Loom and yarn needle.

**Finished Size:**
18" circumference

**Notes:**
*Flowers are made in the round.
*Flowers are made separately and tied into a separate I-cord.
*I-cord is made very long to be wrapped around arm 2-3 times. A shorter cord can be made and tied together instead.

*Working Yarn means the yarn coming from the small ball of yarn in your supplies.

*Work the stitch or "knit over" simply means to lift the bottom loop over the top loop and peg to make the stitch.

### Flower Directions (Make 3) – Use Color B
To begin you need to put yarn loops onto the loom. This is called casting on. The abbreviation is CO.

To start, secure the yarn to the anchor peg with a **Slipknot**.
Place the slipknot on the anchor peg and tighten gently. Do not make it too tight

because later you will release the slipknot after you have knitted a few rounds.

Next you will put a series of loops on the loom to begin knitting. The basic cast on method for loom knitting is called the **E-wrap Cast On**.
Move the working yarn to the inside of the loom between the first and last pegs. Wrap the yarn around the first peg in a clockwise direction.

Repeat for the second peg and all the way around the loom. Make sure you don't wrap the yarn too tight because if you do, it will make it difficult to remove the loops as you work.

This technique is called E-wrap cast on because the wrapped pegs resemble a series of cursive lower case "e's".

**NOTE:** The pegs being wrapped in a clockwise motion with the loom being worked in a counter-clockwise direction. In most cases it doesn't matter which direction you work or how you hold the loom. Work however it is most comfortable for you unless a pattern calls for a specific technique.

Push the loops to the bottom of the pegs.
Wrap all pegs a second time starting with the first peg and ending with the last peg. Make sure you wrap in the same direction as you did the first time. You are now ready to begin knitting.

Hold the working yarn with the same hand that is holding the loom (or you can temporarily secure it to the anchor peg).
Beginning with the last peg wrapped, use your loom tool to lift the bottom loop over the top loop and knit off the loop. (There is a groove in each peg that helps to guide the hook.)

Continue around the loom by working peg 1, peg 2, etc. When all the pegs are worked you will again have only one loop on each peg.
For this flower pattern wrap only 1 more peg and knit over, release the beginning slipknot from the anchor peg.

**Gathered Bind Off:**

Wrap your working yarn (Color B) around the loom 1 1/2 times and cut the working yarn. Thread the yarn onto a yarn needle. (A contrast color yarn was used in the photo for clarity.)

Starting with peg 1, insert the needle below the loop and pull the yarn through. Insert the needle into the loop on the next peg and repeat. Repeat in all the pegs around the loom. Insert the needle into the first loop again to make sure there is no gap. DO NOT REMOVE FROM LOOM YET.

Using Color A, measure around the loom 1 1/2 times and cut. Starting at the first peg use Gathered Bind Off method and work yarn through loops on pegs until all have Color A through them. This strand will be used to tie into and match your I-cord. You should have 1 tails coming from the last peg and 2 from the first peg; hold these two tails as 1 tail.

Remove the loops from the pegs. Being careful not to twist the knitting into the circle, pull the yarn tails until the opening is completely closed. Tie tails in a knot to keep it closed. Trim Color B tail, but not too short.

Using Yarn needle, weave in the beginning yarn tail of Color B into the flower edge. Leave Color A yarn tails long, see Finishing instructions below.

**I-cord Bracelet Directions (Make 1) – Use Color A**

Cast on 3 stitches using the E-wrap method.
Pass the working yarn behind the three cast-on stitches back to the beginning.

Hold the yarn in front of the pegs and knit off each stitch (do not e-wrap!).

Repeat these steps for 18" (inches) or about 72 rows. As you work you will see a tight tube being formed.

To end, move the loop on peg 2 to peg 1 and knit off. Move the loop from peg 1 to peg 2. Move the loop from peg 3 to peg 2 and knit off.

Cut yarn leaving a 6 in. tail and pull through the last loop. Tie the two ends together with a knot. Weave in ends in center of tube with yarn needle.

**Finishing:**

Find the center of the bracelet. Using yarn needle in one tail of a flower, push through a few stitches in the middle. Tie the two tails together tightly and make a knot. Trim off tails. Tie on and knot the next to flowers. On the sample we placed the flowers about 4-5 stitches from the middle flower. Weave in tails.

# Bulky Moss Beanie

A "Jumbo" stitch type pattern Bulky Moss Beanie {Bulky Moss Cowl} Make a Jumbo Stitch skull cap with the Bulky Moss Beanie. This pattern can also be used for a cowl as well; notes for cowl are in "{ }". Need 4-6 Zippy looms and 1 set of Zippy corners.

**Beginner / Débutant / Novicecia**

**Note:** *You can also make this hat on other looms that can knit in- the-round. Use a peg count that is divisible by 4. To make yours, in extra jumbo stitches, use two pegs as one. Mark pegs with a small rubber band, connecting two pegs if you need a visual reminder. The 48 peg 5/8" gauge type loom works best for that (Think CinDwood alternate, old purple KK or Horizon Laptop Knit). It will give you 24 pegs instead of the 20 in this pattern. Standard stitch size, use a multiple of 4 pegs on each peg; any size circular loom.*

## Loom(s):
• 4 KB Zippy looms {Need 6 for a cowl}
• 4 KB Zippy corners

## Yarn:
Super Bulky #6 yarn. Lion Brand Hometown USA was used in sample. 1 skein {2 for a cowl}. Do not use a chenille type yarn for brims as it will not be elastic enough on Jumbo stitches.

## Abbreviations:
- K- Knit (flat knit all)
- P- Purl
- Bet - between
- WY - Working Yarn

## Notes:
*Connect all parts together "in the round". Make sure all zippy peg grooves are facing outward. It will look like a square. HINT: First connect 3 Zippy looms together with all four connectors. Place 4th zippy loom on last by sliding it into place on the last two connectors at the same time.
*This hat uses the full stitch pattern to the edge of the brim for a seamless skull cap design. Alternate brim for pattern - If you want a "brim" look I suggest a 4-row brim of knit 2, purl 2.

## Notes on marking set-up:
The zippy pegs are large and stitch markers are too small. You can tell the first peg if you start the slipknot on a zippy face and notice the tail hanging down as a visual "marker". Also, you can use a small rubber band around the base of the peg, a piece of yarn, or place a piece of tape on the loom base in front of the peg. Use this technique, marking two pegs as one, to adapt it for other looms to get the same look!

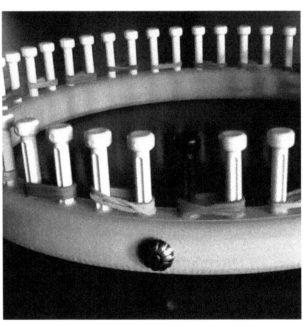

## Best cast-on for Jumbo stitch look:
Cast on all 20 (28) pegs by e-wrapping all pegs ONE time then flat knit all pegs in round.

*All Knits are <u>flat knit</u>[138] in main pattern.

**Round 1: *K2, P2*, repeat bet *,***
**Round 2: *K2, P2*, repeat bet *,***
**Round 3: *P2, K2*, repeat bet *,***
**Round 4: *P2, K2*, repeat bet *,***
**Repeat Rounds 1-4 seven times.**
Repeat Round 1-2; hat should be 8" {rep rounds 1-4 for cowl length}.
See next page for chart and bind offs.

Chart columns (left to right): 20 19 18 17 16 15 14 13 12 11 10 9 8 7 6 5 4 3 2 1

Rows numbered 34 (top) down to 1 (bottom).

**Key**

|  |  |
|---|---|
| ☐ | Knit / k / (RS) Knit |
| ▬ | Purl / p / (RS) Purl |

---

## Mod. Gathered bind off[139]: {cowl - stretchy basic bind-off[140]}

Measure WY around loom 1 1/2 times. Cut WY.

**Round 1:** Purl gather bind off all odd stitches. To begin, *Place WY below 1st peg loop and pull all of tail through loop. Take loop off peg. Place WY behind 2nd peg.* Move on to the next stitch and repeat between *,* for the remaining round.

**Round 2:** Knit gather bind off all even stitches. To begin, *Place WY above 1st peg with loop and pull all of tail through loop. Take loop off peg. Place WY behind 2nd peg.* Move on to the next available stitch and repeat between *,* for the remaining round.

Turn hat inside out and tighten the stitches. Close hat by tying a knot and weave in remaining tails. Turn hat back right side out.

# Easy Fingerless Mitts

**Easy / Facile / Fácil**

**Loom:**
Knitting Board Sock Loom 2 or 3/8" gauge adjustable loom. Could also use the AllnOne loom.

**Yarn:**
Original pattern calls for worsted weight, Aran or 10 ply. A Bulky was used in samples - Cascade 128 Superwash Multis 114 Grapes 1 skein.

**Sizing:**
Pattern written for women's size. For larger mitts follow numbers in (*). **

**Abbreviations:**
• CO - Cast On (Longtail CO: video[141])
• K - Knit or U knit (watch video[142] at min 2:59)
• P - Purl (watch video[143] at min 2:35)
• HH- Half Hitch (video[144])
• BO - Basic Bind off (video[145])
• Longtail CO 32 (36)
•

**Rib section:**
*K2, P2* rep between *,*
Knit 10 (12) rows of ribbing
Knit 20 (both sizes or 24+ for larger hands or desired length) rows

**Thumb section:**
Round 1: K2, BO7 (8), K to end of row
Round 2: K2, HH 7 (8), K to end of row
K 5 (7) rows

**Rib section:**
*K2, p2* rep between *,*
Knit 5 (both sizes) rows of ribbing

BO in pattern*. Binding off in pattern in basic bind off by knitting the knits in the ribbing and purling the purls.
Finishing use a tapestry needle to weave in ends.
Make 2

**Note that sample made in regular size fits a youth of age 8 comfortably shown on model in photography. Sample also fits me but would be more comfortable in larger size with
longer body length. My hands are larger like a man's (knuckles 8" circumference). Use as a guide of making for a man or larger mitt.

# Simple Scarflet Neck Warmer

Button up with this no purl ribbed Scarflet! Change the look of each Scarflet you make by changing the buttonhole placement. Make it asymmetrical, as pictured, or make a shortened neck warmer with a line of 4 buttons for a bold look and warm accessory. Directions for making into a circle for a cowl included.

**Easy / Facile / Fácil**

**Loom(s):**
Sample tested on Knitting Board Basics loom (found in the Loom Knitting Basics Kit); it is 7/16 gauge. Can use any knitting board or long loom at min 3/8''gauge to 3/4''with minimum 1 cm spacing between boards. May need to adjust yarn size or number of strands for gauge. Use AllnOne for wider scarflet or cowl; Cast on more repeats.

**Finished Size:**
4''x 24''(unblocked)

**Gauge:**
Not important; just use an appropriate weight yarn for your loom for an e-wrap stitch.
The spacing between both boards on above loom is a bit wide so between ribs the gauge will be a bit more open

**Yarn:**
Worsted or Bulky. Less than 1 skein. Red Heart Boutique Unforgettable color Petunia was used in sample. It was nice and lightweight.

**Buttons:**
2 –1'' (inch) buttons

**Abbreviations:**
- FB – Front Board
- BB – Back Board
- CO – Cast on
- EW – EW
- Sl – Slip stitch
- St(s) – Stitch(es)

**Instructions:**
Cast on 20 pegs in e-wrap cast on in the following pattern (see illustration).

FB: Double EW CO 4 pegs (e-wrap each peg twice on 4 pegs on front board).
BB: Skip pegs 1-2. Cast on 3 pegs. (e-wrap pegs 3-5 on back board as before).
FB: CO 3 pegs
BB: CO 3 pegs
FB: CO 3 pegs
BB: CO 4 pegs

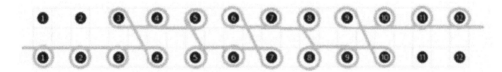

[Loom wrap set-up above: Illustration courtesy of Charity Windham]

**Main pattern:**
Use Slip Stitch flat panel method on all rows. (See example video[146])

Row 1: EW remaining stitches once, in the pattern above, and knit over. Repeat Row 1 till length is approximately desired length. Your knitting will look like 3 columns of ribs; the reverse is identical if item flips. I suggest placing your knitting around your neck to see where it falls and you will want the free end of the scarflet to hang. (My sample was138 rows).

**Add buttonholes:**
Choose pegs you want buttonholes placed and move those stitches over to the adjacent peg. (Sample bound off pegs 3 and 9; as wrapped sequentially on loom). E-wrap the entire row one more time. Work stitches.
Repeat Row 1 again 1 time.

**Bind off:**
Stretchy bind off. (video[147])

**Finishing:**
Add buttons where desired for an a symmetrical look.

I sewed sample buttons on in the following positions.
Button one (opposite buttonhole side of peg 3) is 6.5 inches in from opposite end.
Button two (opposite buttonhole side of peg 9) is 5.25 inches in from opposite end.

**Alternate:**
Use loom knitting Kitchener stitch notes as below to connect as a cowl. See video link for additional help.
An easier method is to use the Russian grafting technique with a crochet hook; it navigates back and front working each stitch. Use knitting needles of a smaller size than
your loops just to hold the stitches. See end of the linked video (see endnotes)[148] of the hexagon blanket for this technique. Start at minute 24:40.
As always in grafting there will be a half stitch jog. You can also sew your ends together with a tapestry needle and matching yarn.
Weave in tails.

# Triple Flip Scarf

The loom knit Triple Flip Scarf is a simple stitch pattern repeated until it reaches long enough to wrap around your neck 3 times and still be loose. Wear as an infinity scarf or a stacked cowl.

**Easy / Facile / Fácil**

### Loom(s):
Sample tested on AllnOne Knitting Board at 1 cm setting. Can use any knitting board or long loom at 3/8″ gauge to 3/4″ may need to adjust yarn size or number of strands to eliminate gaps. New Sock Loom 2 would be the same gauge (3/8″) and smaller, less bulky loom choice for this small width pattern. The new Basic loom from KB basics kit would be nice and lightweight as well but is a slightly larger gauge (7/16″).

### Gauge:
Not important; just use an appropriate weight yarn for your loom for an e-wrap stitch.

### Yarn:
242 yards Sport or Worsted Weight. Samples shown: 2 balls Vanna's Choice color Purple Mist Worsted weight used in sample; heavier for cooler weather. 1 ball Red Heart Shimmer color Snow; it was nice and lightweight.

**Abbreviations:**
- FB – Front Board
- BB – Back Board
- CO – Cast on
- EW – EW
- Sl – slip stitch
- St(s) – stitch(es)

**Instructions:**
Cast on 20 pegs in e-wrap cast on in the following pattern (see illustration).

FB: Double EW CO 4 pegs (e-wrap each peg twice on 4 pegs on front board).
BB: Skip pegs 1-2. Cast on 3 pegs. (e-wrap pegs 3-5 on back board as before).
FB: CO 3 pegs
BB: CO 3 pegs
FB: CO 3 pegs
BB: CO 4 pegs

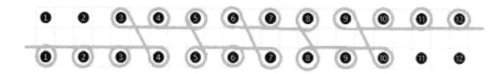

[*Loom wrap set-up above: Illustration courtesy of Charity Windham*]

**Main Pattern:**
Use Slip Stitch flat panel method on all rows. (See example video[149])

Row 1: EW remaining stitches once, in the pattern above, and knit over.

Knit till length is approximately 90′ long with the working strand on the last peg (#20). Leave at least 1 yard of working strand and cut. Sample used 2 balls and ended at 500 rows of triple knit stitch (looks like 3 columns of ribs; the reverse is identical if item flips). *Bind off method options: Kitchener, Russian graft or sew.*

**Setup for bind off:**
Leave live stitches on loom. Slide knitting needle on beginning end of panel. Fasten beginning end and live ends together using Kitchener method. Can transfer loom to needles to use needle Kitchener method or choose loom method by doing the following: use scrap yarn or cable needle to move live loom stitches to front board in order of stitches. Now place beginning end of panel on back board making sure to come up through the middle of the loom and placing all 20 stitches back on the loom onto the back board.

Use loom knitting Kitchener stitch notes below. See the video[150] for additional help.

**Alternate:**

An easier method is to use the Russian grafting technique with a crochet hook; it navigates back and front working each stitch. Use knitting needles of a smaller size than your loops just to hold the stitches. See end of the the linked video (see endnotes)[151] of the hexagon blanket for this technique. Start at minute 24:40.

As always in grafting there will be a half stitch jog. You can also sew your ends together with a tapestry needle and matching yarn.
Weave in tails.

Have fun playing with ways to wear your loom knit triple flip scarf. You can also stack them to look like a taller and thicker cowl as well or infinity scarf.

# Slouchy Newsboy Hat

**NOTE:** This loom knit pattern is meant to be worn with the slouchy part pushed back and patted down and the sides pulled down over the ears. If not worn that way, it has a very "stovetop pipe" look. You can eliminate an added section to have a snugger hat; this optional section is indicated below**. This is warm hat but is light enough to not be restrictive and gets some air flow.

**Easy / Facile / Fácil**

### Loom(s):
Purple 48 peg Knifty Knitter (smaller gauge for adults) 24 Peg Knifty Knitter for optional 2nd decrease. (Photo in above left shows double decrease).
**Optional for less slouchy or tall hat leave out the extra section marked with (* *) below and move on the finishing rows and decrease.

### Yarn:
#6 Super bulky. 2 skeins of Hometown USA by Lion Brand Super Bulky #6 - 64 yards ea. And a contrasting color for accent trim to be crocheted (optional)

**Sizing:** fits adult but is very generous for slouch or lots of hair. For a smaller head or Youth, in the main body of the hat, use a flat or a U knit stitch instead of E-wrap; also eliminating the slouch section will shorten height.** We suggest for a Men's Newsboy hat only eliminate the slouch. For alternates loom sizes, visor formula, and crown decrease see ALTERNATES on the last page of the pattern.

**Abbreviations:**
- EW = E-Wrap
- P = Purl
- SS = Slip Stitch or leaving the beginning peg alone when starting that row
- INC = Adding increased wrap on outside of flat panel. How to video on earflaps here: http://youtu.be/e7YbRLQXTXg
- P2tog: Purl 2 together - Video[152]
- Decreased crown: Video Part 1[153]
- Decreased crown: Video Part 2[154]
- YO: Yarn Over - Video[155]
- Chain CO: Chain Cast On – (erroneously called crochet cast on but Video here to demonstrate technique). Video[156]
- KO: Knit Over the wrapped stitches (also called work the stitch)


CAST ON & "SETUP for ROW 1": Visor Video[157]
*CORRECTION, I added 1 more EW on purl rows which is NOT in the video, depending on the yarn used the edge may look jagged on this side if you do not use an extra EW due to the double increase.

Chain CO starting at 5th peg 16 stitches. Peg 5-20. Work back to left in EW to 5th peg.

## NOTES FOR NUMBERING LOOM:
Peg 1 is the first peg to the right (or counterclockwise) to the end or starter peg. A notation of peg #5 is the peg to the right. This is for starting purposes of the brim.

*VISOR BRIM or SHORT BILL (increasing by 2s):
Row 1: SS, EW 2, Purl 12, EW (16 pegs total)
Row 2: SS, EW 15, add 2 INC. (18 pegs)
Row 3: SS (it's the last INC you added), EW 2, Purl 15, add 2 INC (20 pegs) Row 4: SS (it's the last INC you added), EW 19 (using 20 pegs total)
Row 5: SS, EW 2, P 16, EW 1 (20 pegs)
Row 6: SS, EW 19, add 2 INC (22 pegs)
Row 7: SS, EW 2, P 19, add 2 INC (24 pegs)
Row 8: SS, EW 23 (24 pegs) FINISHED WITH VISOR

CO FOR REST OF HAT:
Row 9: SS, EW 1, P 21, EW, chain CO rest of pegs up to peg 48, *correction: place last loop on peg 1 or ladder will show long. Knit over this stitch first before moving on to the body of the hat.

BODY OF HAT: Work in the round
Row 10-11: EW
Row 12: p
Row 13-14: EW
Row 15: *P 1, P 1 then place on peg before.* repeat till 24 pegs have 2 loops.
Row 16: *P2tog, EW YO*, rep (you've already moved your loops over for the p2tog) [see video[158]]
Row 17-19: EW
Row 20: *P 1, P 1 then place on peg before.* repeat till 24 pegs have 2 loops.
Row 21: *P2tog, EW YO*, rep
Row 22-24: EW
Row 25: *P 1, P 1 then place on peg before.* repeat till 24 pegs have 2 loops.
Row 26: *P2tog, EW YO*, rep

*OPTIONAL STANDARD NEWSBOY style (left photo): If a non-slouchy desired; omit rows between parenthesis "(...)" below.
(*Row 27: EW
Row 28: EW
Row 29: EW
Row 30: *P 1, P 1 then place on peg before.* repeat till 24 pegs have 2 loops.
Row 31: *P2tog, EW YO*, rep *)

FINISH HAT BODY: Row 32-34: EW
Row 35: P
Row 36-37: EW

STARTING CROWN:
Decrease Step 1 (video[159]):
Divide pegs into sections of 6 pegs (8 sections). Decreased beanie: Divide pegs into four sections with markers at every 6th peg.
Round 1 move peg loop 2 to 1 and KO in each of the 8 sections. EW all leftover pegs and KO Round 2: move peg loop 4 to 3 and KO in each of the 8 sections. EW all leftover pegs and KO Round 3: move peg loop 6 to 5 and KO in each of 8 sections. EW all leftover pegs and KO. You should have 24 pegs left.

Decrease Step 2 (Optional but makes a flatter "top" or crown see above photo) [video[160]]:
Use some scrap in a contrasting colored yarn to weave through live loops. Take off the 48-peg loom to transfer to 24-peg loom and take out scrap yarn.

Divide loom into 4 sections of 6. Decrease as on loom above.
Divide pegs into four sections with markers at every 6th peg.
Round 1 move peg loop 2 to 1 and KO in each of the four sections. EW all leftover pegs and KO Round 2: move peg loop 4 to 3 and KO in each of the four sections. EW all leftover pegs and KO Round 3: move peg loop 6 to 5 and KO in each of four sections. EW all leftover pegs and KO. You should have 12 pegs left.

BIND OFF: Drawstring or Gathered BO. And tie off. Weave in tails.

DECORATIVE KNOTTED TRIM (see picture):
In a contrasting color yarn chain 140
Weave thru the first set of P2 tog eyelet spaces. Find an opening to connect the chains with a decorative knot. Weave the ends of the chains and tie a knot on the ends of both to complete. (Make chain longer and tie into a bow, or frog part of chain to shorten decorative knot. You can also connect the ends together to leave out the decoration and just have a chain trim).

ALTERNATES: For alternates loom sizes, visor formula, and crown decrease select appropriate loom for desired size and select appropriate yarn for loom type (if smaller gauge use smaller weight yarn). For Visor determine total peg count (TPC) and divide into 3. That number will be your Visor CO peg count. Formula read TPC /3 = VCO. For example the above loom would read 48/3=16. Now divide your original total peg count (TPC) for your hat into 2. That number will be the final peg count for your increases on the visor (VINC). Formula read TPC/2=VINC and the above hat would be 48/2=24. Cast on in the VCO and increase evenly till reach the final VINC number. The above hat was increased 2 pegs on each side at once but on smaller TPC looms you may only want to increase 1 peg on either side at a time. This was done by 2's to keep the brim short. Smallest size knit was for a 14 month old baby boy. We eliminated the slouch section and used the Martha Stewart loom with large gauge setting on the two semi-circular pieces.

# Dew Drop Shawl

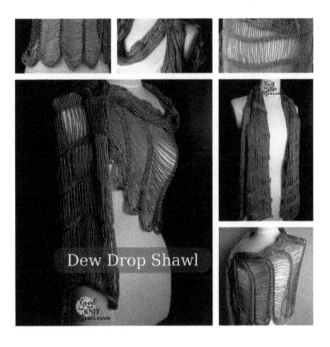

A sleek and glamorous shawl reminiscent of hairpin lace. Change the look with your yarn choice! Go from a dressy date shawl in a shimmery yarn to a casual sock weight yarn or art yarn. Wear as shawl or a keyhole scarf! Impress the ones you love when you wear the Dew Drop Shawl or give as a present.

**Easy / Facile / Fácil**

## Loom(s):
Authentic Knitting Board All-n-One loom. Loom configured at maximum with the 5 peg sliders on ends between the 48 peg front board & 48 peg back board. Could use alternate loom if can configure as above in 3/8" gauge. (Martha Stewart loom with 4 corner pieces and small pegs in all holes works well).

## Yarn:
300 yards of medium weight yarn for shawl or 200 yards if stopping for smaller scarf. Yarn used in test is Sensations Enchantment Silver Metallic. Other test yarns were sock weight and bulky art yarn which gives a totally different look.

## Finished Size(s):
21" x 60" shawl or knit 10-12" for a scarf only

## Abbreviations:

- EW – E-wrap
- BB – Back Board of loom
- FB – Front Board of loom
- St – stitches

(VIDEO for the Dew Drop. Link in endnotes or simply click in eBook.[161])

## Pattern Notes:

We're using the back board (BB) as a place for a holding peg to work the drop stitch and all knit stitches are worked on the front board (FB). Do not skip pegs on FB. The sliders provide the space and no extra wraps are needed for the drops. Plus the width of the shawl actually is the width of the board. It's a multiple of *3 + hold* +3.

The basic pattern is e-wrap 3 & Hold on BB 1 peg behind 3rd e-wrapped peg, EW 3 & hold on BB, repeat pattern till last 3 stitches and EW.

Row 1: *EW 3 on FB, wrap BB1*, repeat between *,* till last 3 sts. EW 3. Repeat Row 1 for 100 rows to knit the maximum intended size or till 21'' measures on ends.

## Notes on sizing:

Work in a flat panel with a turning peg (the first stitch of each row is always slipped, meaning skip and move to peg 2) until SIDE length measures 21'' or length from nape of neck to waistline. The middle will measure longer because of the dropped stitches weight.

For petite shawl measuring 12"x54", as on my test in the sock weight seen below, Use a multiple of 4. Cast on 3, wrap holding peg, *EW 4 on FB, wrap BB1*, repeat between *,* till last 3 st. EW 3. This will take out a few drops and changes the sizing.

The pattern is railroaded by knitting the length, of the shawl, on the actual width of the board (the longest measurement). Knit fewer multiples on any loom and skip 2-5 pegs before wrapping EW to get the same results and it will effectively "turn" it to the side. You would just knit till you got the desired length. For example using a Knifty Knitter: work as a flat panel and skip enough pegs to make about a 4'" drop, then wrap the next peg. Leave 3 pegs at the end to finish the row in 3 EW. Knit till desired length.

## Bind off:

Make sure you have at least 9-10 yards left on ball or skein to bind off (or 3.5 times the length of the loom following around the pegs on front & back). Loose Slip knot bind off, making sure to yarn over around the holding pegs following the pattern it makes along the loom so bind off matches cast on drop stitches.

*If your yarn isn't very nubby you can use my stretchy bind off but you will need to add extra wraps or chains between to span the distance between the drops; this changes the look of the edge to look crocheted which was not intended.*

**Alternate Bind Off:**
(For Dew Drop only)
You can also slip a small piece of matching yarn through the 3 stitches and make a flat bind off or gathered. Tie off and repeat on the other sets of three.

**Optional Fringe:**
Add fringe to both shorter ends as desired OR one of the longer sides to hang from back of shawl.
Sensations Enchantment Silver Metallic (388 yards in ball – 300 yards used) 21" x 60" full size
Weight: 4 – Medium. 5 ozs. 142 gms. 388 yards. 355 meters. 92% Acrylic, 8% Polyester.
Lucci Melange Sunset Romance (216 yards in ball – all yardage used) 12-14" x 60" smaller
Weight: Bulky. Merino Wool, Pima Cotton, Angora, Rayon, Sequins, Metallic, Acrylic, Nylon
TEST in sock weight!
Sensations Enchantment Bamboo & Ewe color discontinued (262 yards in ball – 200 yards used) Petite size
Sock Weight: 40% Wool, 30% Nylon, 15% Rayon. 2.12 oz, 60 grams, 262 yards, 260 meters.

# Bobble Button Newsboy hat

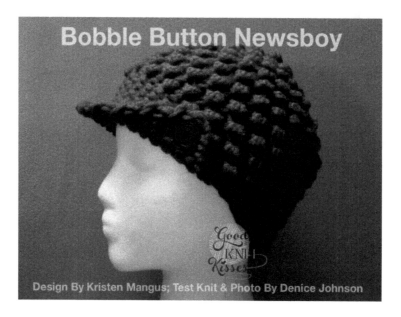

Pattern was inspired by Yarnspirations Women's Peaked Hat in The Crochet Crowd's "Crochet Challenges". Converted to a knit design, his hat features the seed stitch and a field of bobbles with decorative buttons to the visor.

Intermediate / Intermédiaire / Intermedio

## Stitches and Special Techniques Used In This Project:
- CO - True Cable Cast On Video[162]
- HS - Half Stitch (Wrap yarn to outside of row; bring to front of & knit Video[163])
- EW - E-wrap (Video[164])
- K – Knit (Use U-knit stitch Video[165]) - on Visor & Band only
- P - Purl (Video[166])
- BO - Gather Bind-Off
- MB – Make Bobble (Video[167])
- K2tog – Knit 2 together (Decrease)
- SK – Skip peg
- St(s) – Stitches
- Rep – Repeat
- Alt – Alternate (directions)

## Loom:
3⁄4" XLG loom, Martha Stewart loom used in sample at 40 pegs (CO 27). (Alt Knitting Board Hat loom 3⁄4" peg XLG CP Knifty Knitter or Boye 36 peg CO 25; 3⁄4" XLG or Boye 40 peg 7/8" XLG CO 27; or other comparable loom)

## Materials:
- Approximately 315 yds #4 worsted weight yarn 2 strands held as one in sample. (Original sample made using Red Heart Super Saver, Boysenberry; 2 strands pulled from 2 skeins, used approx. half of each skein. Buy two and make one for a friend!) Or use one strand of bulky weight.
- Yarn needle
- Two 1" buttons
- Stitch marker(s) – Only need for peg 1; Alt mark loom for Bobbles on rnds 1 & 3 in 2 colors. 20 of ea color for bobbles

  (12 min for preemie - 24 peg loom); peg 1 only is 3rd color.

## Finished Size:
Pattern is written for Adult Women.*
*For Alternate sizes use a loom, divisible by 2 in peg count and an appropriate weight yarn for that loom. Cast on 2/3 peg round up to nearest odd number.

## Gauge:
2 sts x 4 rows per inch in main bobble pattern

## Notes:
- Make from Visor up to Crown. Visor works as a flat panel and remaining hat connects and joins in the round.
- Visor is 2/3 the number of pegs for hat peg count; use to substitute another loom peg count or gauge.

## Special Technique:
### Bobble (MB)
EW and knit off 5 times on the same peg. Looking behind peg, pick up stitch from previous row below and place on peg. Work bottom two loops over top loop. This completes one Bobble. Place markers on Bobble pegs for reference as needed; use a different color For Round 1 versus Round 4 to not Bobble placement. (Video[168])

## Directions:
Cast on 27 sts using Flat Panel method from left to right. Place a marker under peg 1. True Cable Cast On works left to right; turn to work back and forth. Work visor in flat panel then connect in the Round. Marker indicates peg 1 each round. EW stitch used to obtain gauge and look. If using "Knit" st at alt to EW, use "reverse purl" version loosely.

## Visor:
Row 1: HS, *K1, P1* rep from *,* to end Row 2: HS, *P1, K1* rep from *,* to end Repeat Rows 1-2 until 2" long (1 1/2" Preemie & Baby) - 20 rows total ending on Row 2; 10 repeats total. Will be on right of loom.

**Band:**
Cast on remaining stitches using True Cable Cast On; be sure to add extra loop to connect in the round and lift bottom loop over top. Continue working in the round. Band Round 1: *K1, P1* rep from *,* to end
Band Round 2: *P1, K1* rep from *,* to end
Repeat Band Rounds 1-2 until 3/4" long (1/2" Preemie & Baby) - 6 rounds total ending on Band Round 2; 3 repeats total.

**Main Hat:**
Setup row: EW
Round 1: *EW1, MB* rep from *,* to end [Alt for less bobbles *EW3, MB* rep from *,* to end; must have loom divisible by 4 for this alternate]
Round 2: EW
Round 3: *MB, EW1* rep from *,* to end [Alt for less bobbles *MB, EW3* rep from *,* to 3 sts remain, MB, EW2; must have loom divisible by 4 for this alternate]
Round 4: EW
Repeat Rows 1-4 three more times (or desired length before crown) - X rows total
{**Option as a Slouchy hat:**
Repeat rounds 1-3 as above}

**Crown - Decrease section:**
Round 1: Move even pegs to odd *K2tog, SK* rep from *,* to end. Round 2: EW (SK empty pegs) Round 3: EW (SK empty pegs)

**Repeat** Decrease Section 2 more times; if odd # on last rep knit as usual 1 over 1. HINT: When moving loops over the ones skipped will not be counted anymore. So when moving "even to odd" pegs it is for the remaining loops.

**Finishing:** Bind off using Gathered bind Off Method. Weave ends and block as needed. Fold Brim of hat at corners straight up (at a 90 degree angle) & sew into place with button on each side as pictured and weave in tails.

# Chic Retreat Cowl

A cowl design full of rich texture that is a feast for the eyes!

**Intermediate / Intermédiaire / Intermedio**

## Materials:
- Loom - 3/8" (SG) gauge adjustable loom able to knit in the round, with min 96 pegs. Authentic Knitting Board All-n-One used in sample.
- Notions - Knitting tool, row counter, tapestry needle & crochet hook for weaving tails

## Yarn:
60 yards of Worsted Weight yarn weight. Red Heart Boutique Treasure was used in sample. 2 skeins used.

## Gauge:
Not important for this project

## Pattern Notes:
All K stitches are flat knit. Pattern is worked with one strand in a counter-clockwise direction (left to right).*Follow along with the entire Loom Along Video[169]*

**Legend:**

| Symbol | Name | Description |
|---|---|---|
| ☐ | **knit** | flat knit stitch |
| ◉ | **purl** | purl stitch |

**Legend:**

| Symbol | Name | Description |
|---|---|---|
| ☐ | **knit** | flat knit stitch |
| ◉ | **purl** | purl stitch |
| ⌘ | **color18** | Figure 8 stitch: *sl, k1, k1 prev stitch* sets of 2 pegs |
| 𝕏 | **k1 elongated twice** | Chain lace stitch: k6 same stitch, see pattern for directions |
| V | **slip** | Slip stitch, holding yarn in back |
| ■ | **No Stitch** | Placeholder – No stitch made. |
| ⌀ | **k1 elongated** | Half hitch |
| ⧄ | **c3 over 3 right** | DROP Stitches each peg: *Ew1 & yo3* each peg, then cross 3 drop over 3 right. |

## Abbreviations:
- CLS - chain lace stitch
- EW - e-wrap
- Fig 8 - figure 8 stitch
- HH - half hitch (e-wrap with WY from bottom)
- K - flat knit stitch
- KO - Knit over or knit off
- P-Purl
- WY - Working Yarn
- YO - yarn over

## Instructions:
Cast on 96 stitches in the round, using the double EW method.
- Rows 1-4: *K3, P1*
- Row 5-6: Fig 8

**CHAIN LACE SECTION**
- Row 7: Chain lace stitch, see directions below

**Steps for Row 7 -**
- *Peg 1: EW and KO 6 times to make a chain. (after peg one only, all repeats
- for this part KO 2 over 1 on the first of the 6 EW chains).
- Peg 2: move loop to peg 3, wrap around peg #2 five times (Don't KO).
- Peg 3: EW and knit off 2 over one. Move the top loop from peg 2 over to peg 3 and KO. Repeat for remaining loops till you have 6 chained (the first EW on peg 3 counts).
- Peg 2 will be empty
- Peg 4: move loop to peg 5

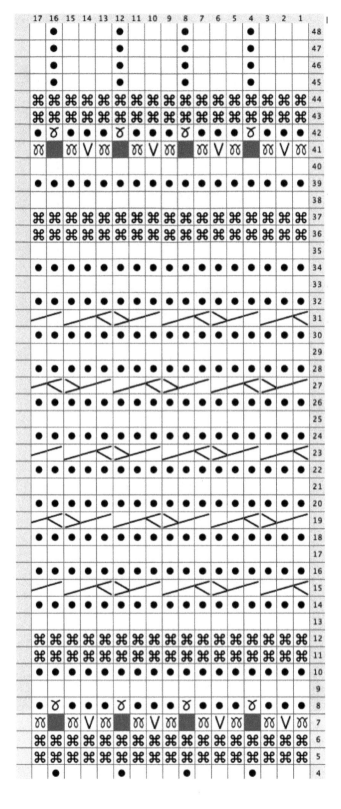

104

- Repeat from * until all pegs have been worked
except peg 96. You will have a ladder yarn behind peg 2 and no ladder
yarn behind empty peg 4.
This pattern repeats from the backside every 4 pegs.
Do not move peg 96. EW & KO 6 times.

- Row 8: Purl. Bring ladder yarns to the front of pegs & purl all. Empty pegs
make a HH.

- Row9:K

- Row 10: P

- Rows 11-12: Fig 8

- Row 13: K

- Row 14: P

**CROSSED DROP SECTION**

*(Five sections with 4 rows each; rows 15-34 will be in this section; see
chart above for graphic and photos. Read Cross Drop stitches SET-UP
carefully.)*

• *Row 15: Drop Stitch pattern as follows: Peg 1 EW & KO then wrap peg
3 times. Repeat
on all pegs. 96th peg it's not needed to wrap 3 times as it will get tugged
down in next step.

**Cross Drop stitches SET-UP**

•Step 1: Pull down drop stitches for entire row and tug on row to guide the drop
stitches to hang evenly. •Step 2: Right cross 3 under 3 all the way around the
loom. The right stitches are picked up with a cable needle and held back. Move
the left 3 stitches to the right 3 empty pegs. Replace the stitches on the cable
needle to empty pegs on the left.

•Row 16: P all drop stitches after they are crossed.

•Row 17: K

•Row 18: P*

•(repeat between *,* for CROSSED DROP SECTION. See notes** below before repeating.

*\*(Repeat drop crossed stitch section 5 times between *,*) Every other time shift over to offset the cables so that the crossed stitches fill the gap from the crossed drop stitches above. Even number dropped rows ONLY will shift over 3 pegs. Work will look like a textured basket weave cable.*

- Row 35: K
- Rows 36-37: Fig 8
- Row 38: K
- Row 39: Purl
- Row 40: K
- Row 41: Repeat CHAIN SECTION. Do not move peg 96. EW & KO 6 times.
- Row 42: P. Bring ladder yarns front & purl. Empty pegs make a HH
- Rows 43-44: Fig 8
- {***Row 44b alternate - add K row if using 150 yard ball change to 2nd ball here. Sample added 1 flat knit row here instead of tie off.}
- Rows 45-48: *K3, P1*
- Bind off with stretchy basic bind off method, same as basic bind off but add 1 EW between bind offs.

# Celtic Knot Cable Scarf

A celtic knot inspired scarf design for a bold and broad statement!

**Experienced / Experimenté / Experiencia**

## Materials:
- Loom - Small Gauge (SG) or 3/8" loom; worked as a flat panel, with at least 42 pegs. Kiss SG loom with no washers used in sample.
- Yarn - About 3 {4} skeins at 242 yds (222 m) of Worsted Weight yarn weight (10 ply UK/AU) or a lighter Bulky (UK/AU 12 ply). 4 Seasons Marvel 12 ply color Grey was used in sample; 222 m per skein (100 grams) = 242 yds. It is as a heavy worsted or lighter Bulky weight yarn.
- Notions - Knitting tool, row counter, cable needle and tapestry needle.

## Gauge:
- 4 sts per inch x 6 rows per inch (stockinette); unblocked
- 2 1/2" long per Celtic Knot Stitch Pattern; unblocked

## Size:
8" x 60" {80"} - Longer men's size in { }; unblocked.

## Abbreviations (see Key):
- K - Knit (U-Knit loosely)
- P - Purl
- c4b - Cable 4 Back
- c4f - Cable 4 Front
- t3b - Twist 3 Back
- t3f - Twist 3 Front
- t4b - Twist 4 Back
- t4f - Twist 4 Front

## Pattern Notes:
All K stitches are u-knit. Pattern is worked with one strand back and forth for a flat panel.
Row 1 work from right to left.
- *Follow along with the stitch pattern* Video[170]. **This is only for the cable stitch pattern and is concise.**
- Follow Stitch pattern Chart for 1 celtic knot.
- Follow large main chart for most of pattern; it is only 9 repeats and shows border (beginning, edges and ending) rows. However, there will be 24 {32} celtic knot repeats to achieve size.

## SEED STITCH PATTERN
Row 1: *K1, P1* across
Row 2: *P1, K1* across
repeat rows 1-2 first and last 4 rows for "End".
repeat rows 1-2 first and last 4 stitches on all other rows for "border"

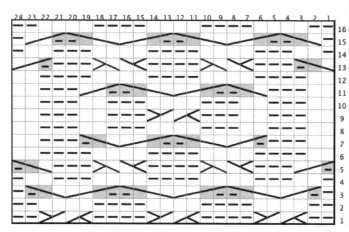

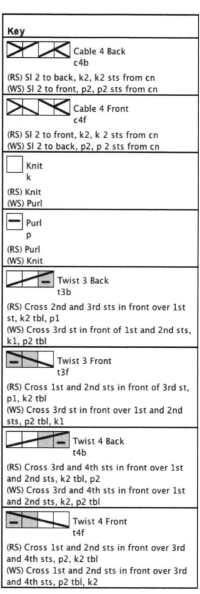

**Key**

| Cable 4 Back c4b |
| --- |
| (RS) Sl 2 to back, k2, k2 sts from cn |
| (WS) Sl 2 to front, p2, p2 sts from cn |

| Cable 4 Front c4f |
| --- |
| (RS) Sl 2 to front, k2, k 2 sts from cn |
| (WS) Sl 2 to back, p2, p 2 sts from cn |

| Knit k |
| --- |
| (RS) Knit |
| (WS) Purl |

| Purl p |
| --- |
| (RS) Purl |
| (WS) Knit |

| Twist 3 Back t3b |
| --- |
| (RS) Cross 2nd and 3rd sts in front over 1st st, k2 tbl, p1 |
| (WS) Cross 3rd st in front of 1st and 2nd sts, k1, p2 tbl |

| Twist 3 Front t3f |
| --- |
| (RS) Cross 1st and 2nd sts in front of 3rd st, p1, k2 tbl |
| (WS) Cross 3rd st in front over 1st and 2nd sts, p2 tbl, k1 |

| Twist 4 Back t4b |
| --- |
| (RS) Cross 3rd and 4th sts in front over 1st and 2nd sts, k2 tbl, p2 |
| (WS) Cross 3rd and 4th sts in front over 1st and 2nd sts, k2, p2 tbl |

| Twist 4 Front t4f |
| --- |
| (RS) Cross 1st and 2nd sts in front over 3rd and 4th sts, p2, k2 tbl |
| (WS) Cross 1st and 2nd sts in front over 3rd and 4th sts, p2 tbl, k2 |

## CELTIC KNOT STITCH PATTERN

Row 1: p2, c4b, p4, c4b, p4, c4b, p2
Row 2: p2, k4, p4, k4, p4, k4, p2
Row 3: p1, t3b, t4f, t4b, t4f, t4b, t3f, p1
Row 4: p1, k2, p3, k4, p4, k4, p3, k2, p1
Row 5: t3b, p3, c4f, p4, c4f, p3, t3f
Row 6: k2, p4, k4, p4, k4, p4, k2
Row 7: k2, p3, t3b, t4f, t4b, t3f, p3, k2
Row 8: k2, p3, k2, p3, k4, p3, k2, p3, k2
Row 9: k2, p3, k2, p3, c4b, p3, k2, p3, k2
Row 10: k2, p3, k2, p3, k4, p3, k2, p3, k2
Row 11: k2, p3, t3f, t4b, t4f, t3b, p3, k2
Row 12: k2, p4, k4, p4, k4, p4, k2
Row 13: t3f, p3, c4f, p4, c4f, p3, t3b
Row 14: p1, k2, p3, k4, p4, k4, p3, k2, p1
Row 15: p1, t3f, t4b, t4f, t4b, t4f, t3b, p1
Row 16: p2, k4, p4, k4, p4, k4, p2
**Repeat rows 1-16 for Celtic Knot Stitch Pattern.

This is the middle 24 stitches. There are **ONLY 9 pattern repeats shown** on chart for visual but knit as many as 24 {32} total repeats to achieve desired length. (See stitch pattern chart for Celtic Knot stitch in detail).

### Instructions

Cast on 42 stitches starting on the left, using the double E-wrap or true cable cast on method; end with working strand on right.

Rows 1-4 **SEED STITCH** End
Rows 5-20 **SEED STITCH** Border, P5,
**CELTIC KNOT STITCH PATTERN,** P5,
**SEED STITCH** Border

*Repeat Rows 5-20 twenty-three (thirty-one) times more for Rows 21-388. {516}
[CELTIC KNOT STITCH PATTERN 24 stitches wide between 4 seed, 5 purl on either side.]*

Last 4 Rows repeat **SEED STITCH** to end.
392 total rows for 60" scarf {520}.

Bind off basic bind off method; loosely. Weave ends with tapestry needle.

# About the Author

Kristen Mangus first learned to crochet as a child from her great Aunt. She discovered finger knitting (closely related to loom knitting) and enjoyed it so much she got in trouble at school for knitting in class! After her fibrous trouble she tried latch hooks and plastic canvas until junior high school. Then Kristen worked with her mom making crafts including homecoming mums, puff paint shirts, jewelry and anything with a glue gun! Kristen's Krafts was born and continued that entrepreneurial spirit into college. She started Angelbearries Floral Designs after working at MJDesigns making tons of bows, floral crafts and wedding florals. Interior Design beckoned. Kristen ended up with a Bachelor of Science degree in Interior Design from Texas Christian University in 1999. For years she enjoyed professionally space planning, forecasting for future challenges, and problem solving with Interior Design. But she was missing her "crafty side" and didn't know it...

Upon experiencing the pains of post-partem, after her third child in 2010, Kristen decided to pick up knitting and crochet books and learn as a form of therapy. The books came in and she studied them and went onward to a late night trip to Walmart. She happened upon a set of Knifty Knitter looms and thought...this looks easier! Having carpel tunnel at the time meant the looms were less strenuous! She found the directions were not so great and was disappointed with the designs. "Why can't loom patterns look like needle versions?!". And so her new journey began. In January 2011 Kristen started the YouTube channel GoodKnit Kisses (known as GoodKnitKisses on YT). It has been quite a journey so far and through having 3 kids, a full time career, an YouTube at night it finally became time to jump all the way. In late August 2014 Kristen took the leap of staying home with her kids and working on GoodKnit Kisses (GKK) full time.

Today GKK has over 137K Subscribers and 20 Million views with people getting the help they need and having fun!

"Getting to be crafty and put Design fundamentals together with my own business has been fantastic but helping others learn and grow to be their crafty best is the greatest gift of all!" -Kristen

## GoodKnit Kisses

**Mission Statement:** To inspire, encourage and empower people through education and design.

1 http://www.goodknitkisses.com/Resources/loom-knitting-guide-and-patterns-2016/

2 goodknitkisses.com/Resources/bo-bind-off-2/

3 https://youtu.be/TpGaPSMMoSA

4 goodknitkisses.com/Resources/co-cast-on-2/

5 https://youtu.be/L0i7d2eqvKI

6 https://youtu.be/CwJ57LmYsNA

7 goodknitkisses.com/Resources/ew-ewrap/

8 goodknitkisses.com/Resources/k-knit-2/

9 goodknitkisses.com/Resources/k-knit-2/

10 https://youtu.be/2KddxbHQyxI

11 goodknitkisses.com/Resources/k-knit-2/

12 goodknitkisses.com/Resources/ew-ewrap/

13 https://youtu.be/L0i7d2eqvKI

14 https://youtu.be/HCjapH8LO_I

15 goodknitkisses.com/Resources/p-purl-2/

16 https://www.youtube.com/watch?v=kr5zOVRt9eI

17 https://youtu.be/eGFnjlFmYF8

18 https://youtu.be/i6fR6_cQYFY

19 https://youtu.be/i6fR6_cQYFY

20 https://www.youtube.com/watch?v=mJZkyU4vpSM

21 https://youtu.be/BIpGEIU0IV0?t=5m55s

22 https://youtu.be/atNiGCpUOTk?list=PLspNyS4jO47zvr6jZmREYOdddrznoPTNa

23 https://youtu.be/HgNMT727w5M?t=1m33s

24 https://youtu.be/BiedDX7mpYM?t=28s

25 https://youtu.be/HgNMT727w5M?list=PLspNyS4jO47zvr6jZmREYOdddrznoPTNa

26 https://youtu.be/jwCuPkd5Vgk

27 https://youtu.be/HgNMT727w5M?t=2m15s

28 https://youtu.be/SZZt6cOFu2Y?t=23m15s

29 https://youtu.be/HgNMT727w5M?t=2m15s

30 https://youtu.be/BiedDX7mpYM?t=28s

31 https://youtu.be/i6fR6_cQYFY?t=3m2s

32 https://youtu.be/kr5zOVRt9eI?list=PL86D25FB98D3A82F8

33 https://youtu.be/s5JbEyr5fNk?list=PL86D25FB98D3A82F8

34 https://youtu.be/CwJ57LmYsNA?list=PL86D25FB98D3A82F8

35 https://youtu.be/BX_0zP-rvQg

36 https://youtu.be/9DR5mN19Mbc?list=PLspNyS4jO47zvr6jZmREYOdddrznoPTNa

37 https://youtu.be/BlpGEIU0IV0?t=5m55s

38 https://youtu.be/9DR5mN19Mbc?t=14m14s

39 https://youtu.be/ii-8OZF5tKU?t=2m54s

40 https://youtu.be/ii-8OZF5tKU?list=PLspNyS4jO47zvr6jZmREYOdddrznoPTNa

41 https://youtu.be/3wH_lkrD9Kw?list=PLspNyS4jO47zvr6jZmREYOdddrznoPTNa

42 youtu.be/RRTfCeiHbVk?list=PLspNyS4jO47xyfnZXpVz5-OGzHR_X4nIk

43 youtu.be/_sTf2tUvAxo?list=PLspNyS4jO47xyfnZXpVz5-OGzHR_X4nIk

44 youtu.be/OZfS0O310vM?list=PLspNyS4jO47xyfnZXpVz5-OGzHR_X4nIk

45 youtu.be/cEN0beJx-FY?list=PLspNyS4jO47xyfnZXpVz5-OGzHR_X4nIk

46 youtu.be/OB2sfQAswfk?list=PLspNyS4jO47xyfnZXpVz5-OGzHR_X4nIk

47 youtu.be/OCFDyz7P9p0?list=PLspNyS4jO47xyfnZXpVz5-OGzHR_X4nIk

48 youtu.be/1gpByeeS2LY?list=PLspNyS4jO47xyfnZXpVz5-OGzHR_X4nIk

49 youtu.be/DHHIW5C0u_g?list=PLspNyS4jO47xyfnZXpVz5-OGzHR_X4nIk

50 youtu.be/GUVivBUDtbs?list=PLspNyS4jO47xyfnZXpVz5-OGzHR_X4nIk

51 youtu.be/dPl73Egm_o8?list=PLspNyS4jO47xyfnZXpVz5-OGzHR_X4nIk

52 youtu.be/05esGw0YHV4?list=PLspNyS4jO47xyfnZXpVz5-OGzHR_X4nIk

53 youtu.be/TIVTH8MI0ec?list=PLspNyS4jO47xyfnZXpVz5-OGzHR_X4nIk

54 youtu.be/KtoLVYL0JeY?list=PLspNyS4jO47xyfnZXpVz5-OGzHR_X4nIk

55 youtu.be/VOND1z3cinM?list=PLspNyS4jO47xyfnZXpVz5-OGzHR_X4nIk

56 youtu.be/MdtQZm9wUE0?list=PLspNyS4jO47xyfnZXpVz5-OGzHR_X4nIk

57 youtu.be/WWDsFlLsrpM

58 youtu.be/w4g84oVcYlc

59 youtu.be/srTwWEGrPSw

60 youtu.be/Ljy5FeKkZF4

61 youtu.be/vquDBXrXs4g

62 youtu.be/myfEBcgmhGk

63 youtu.be/wPAlnC4hfdw

64 youtu.be/Njr2h4aZ240

65 goodknitkisses.com/Resources/stitches-and-stitch-patterns-loom/

66 goodknitkisses.com/Resources/co-cast-on-2/

67 goodknitkisses.com/Resources/bo-bind-off-2/

68 www.youtube.com/playlist?list=PLA914B9AA56C1629A

69 youtu.be/3BUclRuTdh8

70 youtu.be/mJZkyU4vpSM

71 youtu.be/ii4-viJLM24

72 goodknitkisses.com/Resources/k-knit-2/

[73] goodknitkisses.com/Resources/ew-ewrap/

[74] goodknitkisses.com/Resources/p-purl-2/

[75] youtu.be/z3Gx-j59hHk

[76] youtu.be/mFI_IUvk7eY

[77] youtu.be/WTOYNKO2wRs

[78] youtu.be/uDsdfhfxBu4

[79] youtu.be/NWyuunZ8HAo

[80] youtu.be/CwJ57LmYsNA

[81] youtu.be/DwfulOlKT0E

[82] youtu.be/jSsOVIVW6pk

[83] youtu.be/FMIxmt0ywdk

[84] youtu.be/1gvjI0118SY

[85] youtu.be/s5JbEyr5fNk

[86] youtu.be/om9mcG6YJps

[87] http://www.goodknitkisses.com/wp-content/uploads/2016/04/Donations-Checklist.pdf

[88] http://www.goodknitkisses.com/wp-content/uploads/2016/04/Donation-Worksheet.pdf

[89] http://www.goodknitkisses.com/wp-content/uploads/2016/04/Donation-Tax-Log.pdf

[90] www.youtube.com/goodknitkisses

[91] www.goodknitkisses.com/Resources/k-knit-stitch-2/

[92] www.goodknitkisses.com/Resources/p-purl-stitch-2/

[93] youtu.be/OZfS0O310vM?list=PLspNyS4jO47xyfnZXpVz5-OGzHR_X4nIk

[94] youtu.be/cEN0beJx-FY?list=PLspNyS4jO47xyfnZXpVz5-OGzHR_X4nIk

[95] youtu.be/OB2sfQAswfk?list=PLspNyS4jO47xyfnZXpVz5-OGzHR_X4nIk

[96] youtu.be/OCFDyz7P9p0?list=PLspNyS4jO47xyfnZXpVz5-OGzHR_X4nIk

[97] youtu.be/1gpByeeS2LY?list=PLspNyS4jO47xyfnZXpVz5-OGzHR_X4nIk

[98] youtu.be/DHHIW5C0u_g?list=PLspNyS4jO47xyfnZXpVz5-OGzHR_X4nIk

[99] youtu.be/KtoLVYL0JeY?list=PLspNyS4jO47xyfnZXpVz5-OGzHR_X4nIk

[100] youtu.be/VOND1z3cinM?list=PLspNyS4jO47xyfnZXpVz5-OGzHR_X4nIk

[101] youtu.be/MdtQZm9wUE0?list=PLspNyS4jO47xyfnZXpVz5-OGzHR_X4nIk

[102] https://youtu.be/CW_1BZILnIQ

[103] https://www.youtube.com/watch?v=JfsMOIM-wH8&feature=youtu.be

[104] https://www.youtube.com/watch?v=GPX68BOH4_E&feature=youtu.be

[105] https://www.youtube.com/watch?v=2KddxbHQyxI&feature=youtu.be

[106] https://youtu.be/3V0sS4r24J4

[107] https://www.youtube.com/watch?v=atNiGCpUOTk

[108] youtu.be/bfgtCCNXxXs

109 https://youtu.be/ui8hc5-uT4k

110 https://youtu.be/QM03fMImmk0

111 https://youtu.be/ySbNvLvHqsk

112 youtu.be/fkSVxpHuVvE

113 youtu.be/rLAPAGrVhFA

114 youtu.be/WngQN89wAOM

115 youtu.be/2PDcljsLEV0

116 youtu.be/BGav2IXm1-Q

117 youtu.be/2IBM8CbvmNo

118 youtu.be/-Vj0gVpFCGc

119 youtu.be/HCjapH8LO_I

120 youtu.be/pTJIP0PqzIs

121 www.goodknitkisses.com/Resources/dc-double-crochet/

122 www.goodknitkisses.com/marshmallow-crochet-baby-blanket/

123 www.goodknitkisses.com/Resources/loom-knit-stitches-and-stitch-patterns/

124 www.goodknitkisses.com/Resources/loom-knit-stitches-and-stitch-patterns/

125 www.goodknitkisses.com/Resources/loom-knit-stitches-and-stitch-patterns/

126 www.goodknitkisses.com/Resources/loom-knit-stitches-and-stitch-patterns/

127 https://youtu.be/PJmjUHj7P_Y

128 http://www.tsa.gov/traveler-information/prohibited-items

129 www.tsa.gov/traveler-information/transporting-knitting-needles-and-needlepoint

130 https://www.youtube.com/watch?v=HCjapH8LO_I

131 youtu.be/H8GCve7Vm8Q?t=8m3s

132 https://www.youtube.com/watch?v=HCjapH8LO_I

133 https://www.youtube.com/watch?feature=player_embedded&v=YQIehDRvMYA

134 www.facebook.com/groups/loomknitclub

135 www.ravelry.com/projects/estherkate/hand-knitting---writing-patterns

136 www.goodknitkisses.com/wp-content/uploads/2015/04/Magic-Formula-for-Circles-by-Alles-Hutchinson.pdf

137 https://www.youtube.com/watch?v=HCjapH8LO_I

138 https://youtu.be/r5hvRIW3dsM?t=3m24s

139 https://youtu.be/atNiGCpUOTk

140 https://youtu.be/UdNXD7F4tZM

141 youtu.be/OZfS0O310vM

142 youtu.be/r5hvRIW3dsM

143 youtu.be/e7YSLK1v_gU

144 youtu.be/WWDsFlLsrpM

[145] youtu.be/BX_0zP-rvQg

[146] https://youtu.be/cG-m9kimxiM?t=1m1s

[147] https://youtu.be/5z8Gml9DEEg?t=58s

[148] youtu.be/SZZt6cOFu2Y

[149] https://youtu.be/cG-m9kimxiM?t=1m1s

[150] youtu.be/2IBM8CbvmNo

[151] youtu.be/SZZt6cOFu2Y

[152] youtu.be/mJZkyU4vpSM

[153] youtu.be/fkSVxpHuVvE

[154] youtu.be/rLAPAGrVhFA

[155] youtu.be/mJZkyU4vpSM

[156] youtu.be/Njr2h4aZ240

[157] https://youtu.be/ph0FL_MaUm0

[158] youtu.be/mJZkyU4vpSM

[159] https://youtu.be/fkSVxpHuVvE?t=46s

[160] https://youtu.be/rLAPAGrVhFA?t=33s

[161] https://youtu.be/HtnSCz4BNyc

[162] youtu.be/OCFDyz7P9p0

[163] youtu.be/3V0sS4r24J4

[164] youtu.be/HgNMT727w5M

[165] youtu.be/r5hvRlW3dsM

[166] youtu.be/kr5zOVRt9eI

[167] youtu.be/3BUclRuTdh8

[168] youtu.be/3BUclRuTdh8

[169] youtu.be/IF6u-GcIQSg

[170] https://youtu.be/pdhr2qa5_vk

Printed in the USA
CPSIA information can be obtained
at www.ICGtesting.com
LVHW080619011023
759729LV00023B/347